GREEN PROTOCOL

K.B.

Copyright 2022

Zulu23 Performance

The information in this book is designed for people who are participating in or training for physically challenging and sometimes extreme activity. It's not for everyone. Do not use this book or any of the programs within without first consulting a physician. The author and/or any entity involved in the creation or distribution of this book shall have no liability or responsibility to any reader arising out of any injury or damage incurred as a result of the use of the information provided within. The appearance of any U.S. Department of Defense (DoD) visual information does not imply or constitute DoD endorsement.

CONTENTS

SECTION I - GREEN PROTOCOL 1

Green Protocol 2

Combat Fitness 5

On Running & Rucking 12

Overview 15

Structure 17

How To Use 22

SECTION II - SESSION GUIDE 26

Nerd Stuff 27

Sessions 33

    Strength 34

    Conditioning 60

    Deload 86

    Apply a Sense of Play 88

SECTION III - FOUNDATION 91

Capacity 92

    Benchmark 95

    Modifications 96

Velocity 101

    Ultrarunning: Lessons Learned 102

    Benchmark 111

    Modifications 113

    Fueling 119

Outcome 122

    Benchmark ....

    Modifications 128

    Physical Fitness Tests 139

    Train Hard, Fight Easy ....

SECTION IV - CONTINUATION 143

Continuation 144

Continuation Models 147

Long Term Planning – Baseline/Detour 127

Hybrid, Hybrid/Op 150

Concurrent/Combat Arms Template 165

Integrated/Combat Arms Template 169

Block Training 173

Mike India 178

CH 183

FAQs 185

GREEN PROTOCOL

GREEN PROTOCOL

Green Protocol is a strength and conditioning system for a specific type of military athlete: the combat arms soldier. The term 'combat arms' refers to troops that participate in direct ground warfare: the infantry, special operations, armor, like that. This program isn't restricted to the military. It's for any role with a similar fitness profile: tactical law enforcement, smokejumpers, SAR, etc. If you have a need for advanced strength *and* endurance, you're in the right place.

Green Protocol is a hybrid training program. The combat arms soldier is the ultimate hybrid athlete. At the elite end of the spectrum, he needs the endurance of an ultra runner coupled with the strength and structural integrity of a cyborg. These qualities have to coexist to some degree for any combat arms role on the spectrum.

Green Protocol is a comprehensive system designed for every part of your journey. It'll prepare you for entry (selection, bootcamp, schools etc.), for the job itself, and for detours as your goals change and evolve. Training like you're preparing for selection year-round isn't sustainable or desirable. Training like an established team member isn't focused enough for selection or schools.

There are some great 'military' programs out there, but many prescribe too much or too little. They're too complicated or too simple. Some promise elite commando levels of fitness in weeks. This *is* possible – if you have an existing base of similar-kind fitness. Like the British Para looking to move up and try SAS selection. He's spent years on the job and in the field, rucking, running, doing thousands of push-ups and pull-ups, developing a specific kind of fitness and durability that's difficult to replicate in the civilian world. All of it directly applicable to the SAS role. He has a foundation in place. For him, doing a hypothetical '8 Weeks to SAS' program makes perfect sense. It'll allow him to fine-tune his training and make it even more specific to the event. '8 Weeks' becomes a peaking program.

If you're not coming in with a similar background, you might be overwhelmed, overworked, and primed for injury. Intensity is thrown at you immediately in the form of two-a-days, and high-rep/mixed modality workouts. Sessions are too long, and progressions are too quick. If you don't have an adequate foundation in place, there'll be a ceiling on what you can accomplish, even if you make some improvement at first. You're essentially attempting to peak without having the basics in place.

Military fitness is even trickier in that you have to build competence across several disciplines, unlike preparing for a single event like a marathon. 8-12 weeks is barely enough to advance one skill, never mind several. It's too short to have the gradual build-up required to handle the high volume or heavy workloads needed for advanced operational fitness across multiple domains.

The effective approach is to do both. Build a solid foundation in gradual manageable steps, then ramp up the intensity, workload, and specificity. The majority of your time should be spent on foundational fitness. Build a wide and deep base. The wider the base, the higher the peak.

Foundation building takes time. You're probably not going to come across many programs that say, 'for optimal results, first spend 6-12 months working on your strength and running base'. '2 *Years to Airborne Ranger Ninja*' isn't as attractive as '*10 weeks to Airborne Ranger Ninja*'. That's a hard sell. Look at it from another angle… sub in 'Olympic' or 'Professional Athlete'. What sounds more reasonable now? Can you truly become a top calibre performer in weeks? If you're preparing for a high speed role, probably not. Top tier military and police units require just as much discipline, mental fortitude, and physical preparation as their athletic counterparts.

This is where Green Protocol diverges from the norm. It won't turn you into an Airborne Ninja in 8 short weeks. Unless you're already almost there. How long it takes will depend on where you're starting from and how far you need to go. Your Green Protocol might be 3 weeks of peaking, 3 years of immersion, or a lifetime of building mastery.

In the Tactical Barbell system, a Green Protocol is a hybrid strength/conditioning program with an endurance bias. There are many different Green Protocols. This book is a Green Protocol applied to combat fitness. It's an endurance-based program *overall*, although it will include periods of reduced endurance training in order to maximize other attributes like strength and hypertrophy. Don't get hung up on the labels. The labels are used to loosely prioritize and organize training. They're not immutable laws.

COMBAT FITNESS

"Conditioning is the application of fitness"

Joel Jamieson

You can be fit and poorly conditioned at the same time. You might be a top notch cross country runner, but you'll gas out in minutes if you step into the ring with an MMA fighter. Likewise, that fighter might be at the back of the pack in a cross country race. Both extremely fit, but poorly or moderately conditioned for activities outside their sphere of proficiency.

Green Protocol is the application of fitness to military activity.

Training for the 'military' has about as much meaning as 'training for the Olympics' without specifying the event. A soldier in a light infantry unit has a different set of priorities than a military policeman, pilot, or technician. He plays a different sport. The skilled infantry soldier possesses high levels of endurance, along with the ability to execute that endurance over irregular terrain while carrying 70-100lbs of kit. Stands to reason a significant portion of his training is going to involve running, rucking, and getting strong. The military policeman can certainly borrow aspects of infantry training, but the bulk of his time should be spent on domains directly applicable to his trade – like getting bigger and stronger so he can arrest drunk infantrymen on the weekends. The infantry soldier is an ironman/hybrid athlete, the MP a football player or wrestler.

Green Protocol is aimed at the former, which we're going to classify as combat fitness, combat arms fitness, or combat conditioning. Take your pick.

From here on out, when you read the terms 'fitness', 'experienced', 'beginner', etc. it's within the context of combat fitness. You might be an experienced weightlifter, elite even, but in terms of combat fitness you might be a beginner. What holds true when you weight train in isolation doesn't always apply when you add a massive amount of running, rucking, and other event specific training to the mix. It changes the game you're playing. Likewise, If you've been in the combat arms for a few years - you're experienced - even if you need a spotter to bench press an empty bar. Of course, how experienced or inexperienced varies based on the individual.

Let's go a little deeper.

This mission statement is specific to the infantry, but most combat arms trades have a similar role:

'To Close With and Engage the Enemy'

'To Close With' is to get to the objective. In other words, travelling to the jobsite. The commute might consist of a few hundred meters or a few hundred miles. The soldier usually gets to the jobsite on his feet, while carrying everything he needs. He may be inserted closer to the objective by APC, helicopter, or boat, but there's usually some element of foot travel. Getting to work can occasionally be more physically strenuous than the job itself. In many cases, foot patrol for hours or days *is* the objective. This part of the job usually comes down to rucking or moving under load. The things that make you good at rucking and moving under load are rucking, moving under load, running, and strength training.

'Engage the enemy' or perform whatever task has been assigned. That might be CQB, recce, setting up defensive positions, or doing a garbage sweep. More work on tired legs, potentially when the stakes are high. Strength, speed, and work capacity all become important.

You have to be fit enough to get to the problem.

You have to be fit enough to resolve the problem when you get there.

Selections are a great way to get a little insight into combat fitness. They give you a snapshot of what the job entails. A selection is a job interview that can last for days, months, or years. It 'selects' for the ability and aptitude to do the job under extreme physical and mental stress. Bootcamp, hell week, Ranger School, etc. are all selections or components of a selection process.

We're going to look at a couple examples. As you read, think on how you'd train for these events. What would you spend time on? what stops being important, and what might interfere with the stuff that is important?

The British SAS is one of the premier special operations groups in the world. The first phase of their selection process is called 'Endurance'. It's right there in the name. Endurance lasts for approximately a month and involves daily rucking over challenging terrain with loads and distances that progressively increase. Timings have to be met. Often those timings are unknown to the candidates. If you can't handle uncertainty, fuhgeddaboudit. Endurance Phase culminates with several brutal tests. The first is called the 'Fan Dance'. Candidates have four hours to ruck over a mountain in Wales (Pen Y Fan) – twice – while carrying a 40lb ruck plus rifle. The Fan is an 886 meter peak.

The event covers a total distance of 24km. Think of the pace you'd need to sustain with that kind of elevation and load. And the weather - the standards remain the same whether it's summer or winter. Heat exhaustion or iced-over uphill/downhill movement – the choice is yours. Another test known as the 'Long Drag' consists of a 40 mile forced march with a 55lb ruck and a 24 hour time limit. Basically, an ultramarathon while carrying an extra 55lbs on your carcass.

The Fan Dance and Long Drag are nasty feats on their own, but what makes them especially challenging is that they aren't done in isolation. Over the entire month leading up to testing candidates have been rucking and navigating almost daily - anywhere from 10-20 miles or more. They're sleep deprived, stressed, and eating less than perfect diets. The wear and tear has set in. There's more than a few missing toenails, serious blisters, and various tendon and knee issues. When test week arrives, they're most definitely not at their best. If you want a taste of this kind of cumulative physical stress, run 15-20 miles everyday for a month. In the mountains. Run an ultramarathon or two at the end of the month without tapering. Report back.

Let's look to police special operations for the next example. The South African Special Task Force (STF) is a tactical unit in one of the most hostile and difficult places to police on the planet. Approximately 400 officers apply to STF every year. Roughly 20 make it through. One of the final selection stages is called 'Vasbyt'. Vasbyt is an Afrikaans term meaning to 'bite down hard and endure'. Very fitting. Vasbyt is a brutal 4 day torture session designed to test mental and physical endurance. Candidates aren't allowed to eat or sleep for 90 hours and can only drink water when directed by the cadre. Let that sink in. They begin by marching approximately 40km carrying a slab of railroad track with an iron ball hanging off of it. It's impossible to carry comfortably by design. Awkwardly shaped, and very difficult to balance in one position for long. After the forced march the candidates are bombarded with a series of tests and obstacles designed to probe their phobias. Some of the obstacles include traversing a rope strung up high over a river, and swimming across the top of an overflowing dam with no safety in place. After that, it's back to their old friend the iron rail, for another forced march - this time a brutal 70km. All in all, the candidates cover about 200km over the four days. During the entire ordeal they're mocked and encouraged to quit. Many would tap out at the no-food-for-four-days part, even if they just had to lie on a couch and watch Netflix, never mind the rest of it.

The SAS and STF are on the extreme ends of soldiering and policing, but most combat arms units will have a weeding-out process with similar ingredients: sleep deprivation, running, rucking, timings, exposure to the elements, phobia testing, and hard labor. The dose and degree of difficulty will depend on the unit and level of operations.

Whether you're preparing for Tier 1 or conventional infantry, consider how you'd train for that flavor of strength and endurance. Running is the cornerstone of combat fitness – it is second to none for building the type of cardiovascular engine and staying power required for working or moving your body for long periods of time. But you can't *just* focus on running. Adding load and elevation changes the game. Throw a ruck or plate carrier on a prolific marathon runner, put a bunch of mountains in front of him, and watch his performance go down the drain. Injuries shall ensue.

So, just ruck a lot? Ruck all day, ruck all night? Not necessarily. Rucking is hard on the body. Too much rucking adds unnecessary physical stress without a significant accompanying increase in performance. In other words, there's a relatively rapid point of diminishing returns when compared to other forms of training. One of the best ways to break the ceiling and optimize rucking is to become a better runner and increase strength. More on this later.

Speaking of strength, the right lifting program can be the difference between success and failure. High volume workouts that have you consistently annihilate a particular lift or muscle group are going to interfere with all the running, rucking, and conditioning you have to do. As you can see from the examples above, conditioning isn't going to be just a couple days of sprints or sled pulls. You're playing a different game now. Make no mistake, the right kind of strength training is invaluable. Carrying a 100lb ruck on a frame comprised of compact muscle, strong connective tissue, and dense bone will make you far more mobile and injury-resistant. The wrong kind of lifting will leave you beat up, tired, and open to injury. You'll find it difficult to meet your conditioning responsibilities. The ability to apply that strength over a long period of time is extremely important as well: doing hundreds of push-ups over selection, filling sandbags, log PT, or stacking ammo cans.

Running, rucking, and strength training are the foundation of combat fitness. Work capacity sits on top of that foundation. Ultimately, everything we do in this book is designed to increase work capacity.

Think back to the example of the cross-country runner and MMA fighter at the beginning of the section. Should the cross-country runner spend the majority of his conditioning time doing heavy bag drills, sparring, and pad work? Should the fighter spend most of his time and effort on an overly complex running plan that incorporates various distances, thresholds, and intervals? Probably not. Remember, fitness vs conditioning. All of these activities will build fitness but won't translate into optimal conditioning for specific sport. It also takes time away from the training that pays the bills. Doesn't mean other forms of training can't be incorporated. Far from it. Running or roadwork plays an important role in MMA, but it shouldn't eclipse time spent on more fight-specific conditioning drills.

Combat fitness is no different. I saw a question on a forum once. A young man was training for ranger school and asked for conditioning advice. The top answer recommended a barbell based metcon style workout. The kind where you shoot for hundreds of reps, mix in a little cardio like burpees, and try to annihilate yourself. Way down at the bottom, completely ignored, was a suggestion to spend time mostly running and rucking. Not very sexy. Knowing what you know now about combat fitness, hopefully you should be able to figure out which answer was more on point. Is there a place for barbell/metcon/annihilate-yourself work? **Absolutely**. You'll find training like that in this book and in other Tactical Barbell programs. But it isn't necessarily the meat & potatoes when it comes to combat-arms conditioning.

> Running, rucking, and strength training are the foundation of combat fitness. Work Capacity sits on top of that foundation.

ON RUNNING & RUCKING

*'You gotta be **really really** good at running and rucking. You gotta be pretty strong for a long period of time, not extremely strong once.'*

Said in hundreds of different ways by hundreds of successful and unsuccessful selection candidates around the world.

If you're police special operations or similar and do little or no rucking, the information in this section still applies. You're working under load in the form of HBA, breaching tools, etc.

If the combat arms had a sport, it would be rucking. How good you have to be will depend on the unit or role. Infantry soldiers should be able to comfortably ruck with 40-50lbs (plus gear) at a 15 minute/mile pace or faster. When you start venturing away from conventional units the load and pace requirements change. Royal Marines are required to perform a 30 mile ruck with 50lbs in under 8 hours. Speed, load, and distance aren't the only variables. The ability to ruck over challenging terrain is a make-or-break factor. Ranger school candidates are faced with mountainous terrain (sometimes in the neighborhood of 40 degree angle inclines) while carrying almost a hundred pounds of gear.

Rucking more will of course improve rucking, but unlike running or lifting, there's a quicker point of diminishing returns. 1-3 times a week is usually the sweet spot, depending on what you're preparing for and where you are in your training cycle. Beyond that, running and increasing strength will contribute more than just doing more rucking.

The US Naval Special Warfare Centre (sealswcc dot com) is a goldmine of information. They study hundreds of SEAL/spec war troops at various stages of the game. They're a bunch of sports scientists that get to sift through thousands of performance reports containing candidate stats; run times, swim times, points of failure, successes and much more. Patterns emerge. Here's the conclusion they came to after analyzing data from numerous SQT/SOAS candidates:

> 'Rucking requires a combination of strength and endurance…(but) running is the strongest predictor of ruck march performance.'

To get better at rucking, get better at running. Strength training starts contributing more when loads exceed 50-70lbs, or if the load bearer is disproportionately underweight/weaker than average.

To sum up, the best way to optimize your rucking is to ruck, run, and build strength.

So, we've established running is important for rucking. Running is also important for a whole lot of other things. Here's some more data from the same Naval Spec War community:

> 'Endurance (run & swim) is the most important factor regarding the probability of completing Hell Week.'

Running, not 'cardio'. SEAL training has a significant water component, if you're a land based-creature, substitute ruck for 'swim'.

Selection, schools, and operations are endurance games. Running is the gold standard for building the type of endurance required. The amount varies depending on what you're training for, but the higher the tier the more you should rely on getting around on your feet.

Running provides specific muscular-endurance to the legs, core, and other supporting structures. It's the best way to get better at being on your feet. Cycling won't do it. A bicycle displaces too much of your own weight and doesn't provide enough of a stressor to provide the adaptation we need. It's too efficient. As occasional supplementary cardio it's fine, but it shouldn't be your primary mode of training. Same with swimming. Buoyancy offsets bodyweight. Swimming and water-skills are extremely important for amphibious units but shouldn't replace the role of running.

Other than endurance, what should a 'military' runner focus on? The combat arms soldier needs speed. Speed to achieve tasks or objectives in a timely manner. Speed for periodic fitness tests which usually include a timed event like the 1.5 or 4 miler. But it's not enough to have endurance and speed. The combat arms soldier needs the ability to apply that endurance and speed over challenging off-road terrain: elevation, non-existent trails, mud, and gravel. Think you're good to go because you have a 40 minute 10k time on the road? Throw in a few kilometers of steep offroad elevation and watch that time double or triple. Or ask any BUD/S survivor about their first soft sand run. Terrain is a game changer.

OVERVIEW

Green Protocol consists of two phases: Foundation and Continuation.

Foundation is that all-important building phase. We're going to build you from the ground up and install the base required for advanced military performance. That base consists of strength training, running, and rucking. You'll finish Foundation with the ability to run for 20 miles or more, ruck for 20 miles with 50lbs or more, and have the accompanying strength and work capacity required for the combat arms role. Foundation includes a brief peaking block that can be picked up and used at anytime provided you have the prerequisite conditioning in place – our version of '8 weeks to Ninja Commando'.

Foundation can loosely be looked at as entry-level training. What you do to get your foot in the door. Continuation is what you do after you get on your dream-team. You can't train like you're preparing for selection forever. Not only is it too physically demanding and time consuming, but it may not be the right type of fitness for operations and unit life. Selection/schools are generally endurance biased. After selection you might want to slide closer on the spectrum toward strength and muscle depending on the flavor of your unit. Continuation will give you that choice and provide you with several strategies and templates for progressing your newfound fitness at a sustainable pace. There will come a point where you want to try new things and maybe take up a completely different style of training for a while, like kettlebells or Zumba. Maybe you want to focus on one particular domain like hypertrophy or strength-endurance. Continuation includes guidance on creating a baseline plan from which you can take such training detours. Continuation can also be used whenever you're in a holding pattern before selection or school but not close enough to use the Foundation peaking block.

If you don't need to ruck much (or at all) for your particular objective, more relevant sessions can be substituted throughout each phase. Guidance will be provided.

Periodization occurs within each template and over the system as a whole. When strength and strength related domains are prioritized, running is minimized or prescribed at a manageable level of intensity. Likewise, as the mileage and conditioning ramp up, heavy lifting takes a back seat.

STRUCTURE

FOUNDATION

Foundation consists of three templates: **Capacity**, **Velocity**, and **Outcome**. Think of them as your lift, run, and ruck templates, although they are much more. Each is approximately 12-16 weeks and builds on the one that came before it. Each has a recommended benchmark to meet before proceeding to the next. The templates can be abbreviated to meet lower benchmarks and adjusted for those with more or less experience. Experienced trainees can start the templates further in or skip them completely depending on needs and level of fitness. After adjustments, your template might end up being just 4-8 weeks, or even longer than the standard 12-16. Abbreviated and custom programming will be covered in-depth.

The Foundation templates are designed to take you from near zero to three benchmarks or minimums:

1. 20 Mile Off-Road Run - 8 hours or less
2. 20 Mile/50lb Ruck at or near target pace
3. Develop strength/muscular-endurance for the combat arms role

There is no metric applied to strength - this will vary based on the individual's programming choices. The ability to meet the prescribed benchmarks will give you a rock solid physical platform from which to pivot and perform in any combat arms environment with minimal adjustment. You can't train for every little thing, but if you become very good at the important things it's not difficult to improve in other related areas. Water the roots, and the leaves will take care of themselves. Benchmarks are primarily used to ensure the majority of GP trainees are getting basic objective results. Benchmarks are advanced minimums, waypoints on the road to elite combat fitness. Train consistently, and you'll exceed them.

Capacity is a concentrated period of building muscle, increasing strength, and laying a foundation of basic aerobic fitness. It builds general fitness that is later converted into combat fitness. Capacity has a relatively easy 6 mile/60 minute benchmark that has to be met before proceeding to Velocity.

Velocity is a running/conditioning program that picks up where Capacity ends. Velocity is a bastard child of the ultramarathon community designed specifically for the unique needs of the military athlete: endurance, speed, and the ability to apply both off-road. The ultra style of training carries over to rucking, operations, and moving over irregular terrain much more effectively than other forms of run training. The Velocity benchmark is a 20 mile off-road run or a 27 mile challenge.

Outcome channels the raw strength and conditioning you've built into rucking, work capacity, and muscular endurance. The first half focuses on building basic ruck proficiency and work capacity. The second half acts as a peaking or sharpening phase with a built in taper that can be used directly prior to school or selection. The peaking phase of Outcome is challenging. Two-a-days are standard issue, and overall training volume is increased significantly. At this point you'll have Capacity and Velocity under your belt, so it'll be well within your physical capabilities. The final benchmark is a 20 mile ruck with 50lbs or a combined 30 mile ruck/run challenge session.

If your objective isn't ruck intensive, you can skip Outcome or substitute more applicable training sessions. Alternatives will be provided. Rucking aside, Outcome brings value by way of increasing work capacity through two-a-days, and specific sessions like Peggy's Hills. I recommend it even if you're preparing for a limited or no-ruck role like tactical law enforcement.

CONTINUATION

Foundation is a concentrated phase that takes you away from the real world in order to significantly level up. Training becomes your life. It requires a higher than normal amount of work, time, and dedication. That kind of tempo isn't sustainable indefinitely alongside career, family, operations, etc. You have to turn it into your new normal without burning yourself out. Enter Continuation. Continuation is about integrating your newfound fitness and progressing it at a manageable pace.

Foundation is on the rigid side with prescribed distances, exercises, and times. It has specific objectives and is a 'do this' set of plans. Continuation is flexible. It's your everyday long term program. It can be customized and adjusted for your goals, and you'll be able to incorporate other protocols and programs as needed.

Continuation consists of several templates and strategies: Hybrid, Hybrid/Operator, Concurrent/CAT, Integrated/CAT, Block Training, and Mike India. Pick the approach that resonates or best fits your situation and objectives.

Hybrid. Nothing but lifting and running using a simple two-pronged approach. The first half of the template emphasizes lifting, the second prioritizes conditioning. The Hybrid focuses on two core activities that form the foundation for operational fitness. It also works well for those that get other more specialized aspects of fitness through work or play – like unit PT, MMA, and other sports. If you don't get specific fitness from elsewhere, take training detours and incorporate blocks of SE, hypertrophy, or whatever else you need, whenever you need it. Simple, flexible, and effective. **Hybrid/Operator** or Hybrid/Op is a 50/50 variant of the standard version.

Concurrent/Combat Arms Template. C/CAT uses a concurrent approach to combat fitness. All major domains and specialized fitness are trained on a weekly basis. Every training week includes a strength component, rucking, speedwork, elevation training, and long runs. Apart from being a high-speed template, it's great when you're in a holding pattern waiting for selection or school. It keeps your fingers in all the pies at a sustainable tempo.

Integrated/Combat Arms Template. I/CAT takes all three Foundation modules and compresses them in a single, repeatable template. I/CAT loosely employs block periodization. It starts with an emphasis on strength/hypertrophy, tapers into high mileage running/conditioning, and finishes with operationally specific training: rucking, muscular endurance, and work capacity. Then the cycle repeats. For those that want a seasonal or segmented approach, I/CAT is the way to go. A good fit for reserve or guard units.

Block Training is a strategy, not a template. It's used for unpredictable schedules, high-tempo nomadic lifestyles, and/or constantly changing access to equipment. Training is broken down into specialized three-week blocks: Hypertrophy, Strength, and Endurance. Pivot and do the block your situation dictates. If you're in an environment without access to a gym – make lemonade and run an Endurance block. If the situation changes and barbells become available, build muscle or work on strength. All operational athletes regardless of Continuation protocol can employ Block Training as a backup plan when the situation requires it.

The Missing Ingredient aka **Mike India** approach consists of adding only what is missing. If you have a very active lifestyle with mandatory unit PT, organized sport, and/or strenuous day work, adding a full blown strength and conditioning protocol might be a recipe for injury and burnout. Add only the component(s) that your life doesn't provide.

Long term planning, training detours, and incorporating other programs will be covered.

HOW TO USE

"Obey the principles without being bound by them."

Bruce Lee

If you skim over this book, it'll seem complicated. If you take the time to read it, you'll realize how dirt simple it is. The busy looking tables, numbers, and abbreviations will make perfect sense. You'll notice recurring patterns, principles, and instructions. I repeat myself often, one because I'm not Charles Dickens, and two, I want to install some of the important concepts in your head by beating them into you. When you get a solid grasp of the overall program and guiding principles, you'll be able to maximize your results by customizing it for your personal objectives.

I'm going to keep theory to a minimum in this book. It'll be very surface-level. The focus is going to be on the templates and strategies, not on the underlying science of the various energy systems. If you want more than what's provided here, read *Tactical Barbell I* and *II*.

I suggest reading the entire book once before starting. Keep doing your old program or run a Mass block in the meantime. It won't take long. After that initial read-through, come back and reread the chapter/template you'll be using first. Read it carefully and thoroughly.

Have a loose big-picture plan, but don't get too nitty-gritty too far in advance. Focus on the template you're on, because the results might change how you program or customize the next. Don't plan out every single session of Capacity, Velocity, and Outcome before you even begin. Concentrate on Capacity first. Customize it. Work through it. Once you're finished, move on to Velocity and do the same. Use the results and lessons learned from Capacity to adjust or modify Velocity as needed. Repeat with Outcome.

Green Protocol's modular structure makes it extremely versatile. GP is a system, a single program, and multiple programs simultaneously. You can take the pieces, rearrange them, and customize them for your goals. You can start the system at almost any point depending on your existing level of fitness and goals. Want to skip Velocity and use Outcome immediately? If you have the prerequisite fitness, have at it. Already an established team member but looking for long term programming? Skip Foundation entirely and start using a Continuation template. Your Green Protocol might be a 3 week peaking phase, or a one year prep plan. Operational requirements vary. One size fits all isn't a reality.

THE STANDARD APPROACH

Start with Capacity, work through Velocity, and finish with Outcome. Do your school, selection, or event if applicable. Transition to a Continuation template. Take training detours as goals, desires, or roles change. Return to baseline Continuation programming as needed. This is a powerful approach if you're new to combat fitness. It'll ensure you have a rock-solid foundation in place, and you'll avoid wasting years of trial and error.

PLUG AND PLAY

Every single template in this system can be used as a self contained program. Use the individual templates as needed in addition to your regular non-green programming.

Capacity is the perfect general strength and aerobic block to use anytime you feel the need to return to basics: building muscle, strength, and foundational aerobic fitness. Capacity can also be used as an alternative to standard TB Base Building.

Maybe you're using a *Tactical Barbell* protocol like Operator/Black but need a focused running program to prepare for an event. Take a break from Black and work through Velocity. Too easy.

Skip templates if it makes sense. If you're an experienced marathoner you've got the running down but maybe minimal ruck, strength-endurance, and work capacity training. Doing Velocity may not be the best use of your time. Go straight to Outcome after Capacity and channel your established cardiovascular abilities into specific fitness. Outcome acts as a specificity/peaking block for those that already have an adequate strength and running foundation.

FOUNDATION + SPECIFICITY

Do this if you're training for a highly specific event that isn't be covered by GP programming. Use Capacity, Velocity, and Outcome to build high levels of general combat fitness. Then, use a selection or event specific program to peak. For example, if you're preparing for the SEALs, use a SEAL specific program in the months leading up to BUD/S. A BUD/S program will fill in any gaps and prepare you for the exact events you'll face. This approach can apply to anything: obstacle course races, tactical fitness challenges, mountaineering expeditions, PFT prep, etc.

CONTINUATION ONLY

Skip Foundation and begin Continuation. This might be a logical choice if you're already on a team and want a go-to training template for year round use. Also appropriate for recreational or civilian trainees that don't need the immersive training that Foundation provides.

CUSTOM BENCHMARKS/ABBREVIATED PROGRAMMING

The entire program can be modified for lower benchmarks and adjusted for those with more or less experience. If the existing benchmarks are overkill or imbalanced for your particular goals, train for more appropriate numbers. If you're coming in with an existing fitness base, you can start further along each module and cut down on your overall training time. This will be covered extensively, and sample abbreviated templates are provided.

SESSION GUIDE

NERD STUFF

Feel free to skip this section. We're going to take a brief look at how training is categorized and organized. I've covered this in other books, so this will be a shallow dive.

Breaking fitness down into domains helps with programming. It helps prioritize and allocate training time. It helps in other ways as well. Training certain domains before others can be more effective since some rely on others to maximize their potential.

The idea is to take the various domains such as strength, hypertrophy, endurance etc. and develop them to the degree needed for your particular role. We train them in the right order to maximize results. Then we take those pieces and put them together to create the whole picture.

Cardiovascular Fitness. The aerobic system powers almost everything you do and is the energy system that can be improved the most. It can take a human that loses his breath stumbling from couch to fridge, to running a 200 mile ultramarathon. It plays a strong role in events not typically thought of as 'aerobic' or 'endurance' such as the 200 meter sprint and mixed martial arts. It is vital for repeated high intensity efforts because it resets the anaerobic system(s). The fitter the aerobic system the quicker it resets the anerobic system(s). It's the difference between collapsing/gasping for air like a fish out of water after a max effort hill sprint or being ready to do it again in moments. The anaerobic system gives you that quick burst of energy, the aerobic system determines how soon you'll be able to access it again. When it comes to combat fitness, the aerobic system is emperor. It will be the first point of failure if you're not prepared.

The anaerobic systems(s) are your after-burners, they activate when you need energy faster than the aerobic system can provide. Bursts of speed, working at a higher sustained tempo, or the explosive application of muscular force, are all fueled to some degree by the anerobic system(s).

Both systems are important and come together to create your engine. Whether it's a timed run for PFT, rucking to an objective, or working/moving continuously for days at a time, this is your energy source. Combat fitness is endurance based therefore we apply the formula of elite endurance athletes in this program:

High Volume + Strategic Intensity = Success.

Lots of easy mileage, interspersed with the right amount of high intensity training and speedwork. As it applies to combat fitness (don't forget the context!).

Strength. AKA maximal-strength. The ability to generate force. You're probably never going to lift a 300lb keg over your head and throw it at the enemy, but strength is extremely important for the underlying role it plays. Strength makes the body injury-resistant. It builds durability and structural integrity. Vital when it comes to carrying a 100 pound ruck or thundering in like a drunk buffalo after a static line parachute jump. You'll appreciate pull-ups when you're hanging on a caving ladder over the bright blue sea wearing 60lbs of gear. Strength contributes significantly to ruck proficiency when loads exceed 50lbs or if the load-bearer is weaker/lighter than average.

If you can squat 400lbs, that 90lb ruck ain't so bad. Strength is a foundational domain, it increases your capacity for other domains like muscular-endurance, power, and speed. The most efficient way to increase strength is through the use of a structured plan with a methodical progression model. The primary driver of strength training is intensity as measured by load.

Strength-Endurance. AKA muscular-endurance. When it comes to combat fitness, you don't have to be extremely strong once, you have to be moderately strong for long periods of time. SE contributes directly to military performance: rucking, fitness tests, group punishment sessions during selection/school/bootcamp, and tasks associated to your objective. The turnover of leg muscles during a ruck march relies in part on SE. SE training builds work capacity and strengthens muscles, joints, and connective tissue. SE is trained directly and indirectly. Directly by using specific movements and progressions (such as the SE training found in this program) and indirectly through activity. For example, running and rucking will significantly increase the strength-endurance in your legs and supporting muscles.

Work Capacity is used here as a loose catch-all term. It's the ability to execute multiple domains simultaneously. Doing a little bit of everything. A timed obstacle course for example. You're running, using strength, muscular-endurance, maybe some explosiveness, power, and speed. It also refers to the volume of work you can handle. The ability to train 2 or 3 times a day, or over several days continuously (think hell-week type scenarios). Ultimately, everything we do in this book is aimed at increasing work capacity in a combat fitness context.

Other domains include **hypertrophy**, **power**, **power-endurance**, etc.

Power and it's subcategories are trained directly and indirectly in this program. Specific speed/power training is included in the Operator/Daily Undulating Periodization template. It's also trained indirectly by way of speedwork and other conditioning sessions.

Hypertrophy or building bigger muscles is moderately important for our purposes because it supports strength development. Making the muscle larger first, increases the capacity for that muscle's strength. *Excessive* hypertrophy is not desirable for combat fitness because of the endurance component. Excess weight in the form of muscle or fat is like wearing a weight vest or adding another 10-20lbs to your ruck. It forces the heart and supporting energy systems to work harder, leading to fatigue and early cessation of performance. 'Excess' is different for everybody. How much mass you can get away with will depend on your bone structure and build. Like a champion UFC fighter or elite wrestler, the effective combat arms soldier develops the least amount of mass needed for the greatest amount of strength. That said, don't get fixated on some magical target weight. Focusing on some idealized weight/height/ ratio to pass a school is stupid. As you will experience soon enough, successful, and unsuccessful candidates come in all shapes and sizes. Do the training, eat like an athlete, and your body will reshape and adapt for peak performance. The weight at which *you* perform best is unique to you. Form follows function. In Green Protocol, hypertrophy is trained by way of the strength templates, along with hypertrophy-specific programming included for special cases (trainees coming in underweight and/or for those preparing for a role with a lesser endurance component etc.). The primary driver of hypertrophy is volume.

These domains are all loose categories with infinite overlap. The body works as a single unit, not a collection of isolated functions that switch neatly on or off as needed. Don't get fixated on the labels, at the end of the day they're just a programming aid.

ORDER OF OPERATIONS

In the world of classic block periodization, there's a preferred order for training the various domains.

On the strength side of the house:

> **Hypertrophy > Maximal-Strength > SE/Power/other strength subdomains**

Making the muscle bigger first (hypertrophy) increases it's capacity for maximal-strength. Strength training will increase muscle mass sufficiently by itself for our purposes, but specialized hypertrophy work is another way to get a little extra oomph out of it.

Maximal-Strength increases the capacity of other strength domains like strength-endurance and power. For example, doubling your bench press will predictably raise the ceiling on your maximum number of push-ups or other upper body muscular-endurance markers. It doesn't work as well the other way around. Doubling your push-ups won't have a significant effect on your 1RM bench press or ability to generate force. High rep push-ups are a great way to improve strength-endurance, but suboptimal for improving maximal-strength. Max-Strength training is ideally placed after hypertrophy and before strength subdomains like power and strength-endurance.

As above, strength-endurance is a child of maximal-strength. A 2009 study involving trained firefighters determined that developing a higher one rep max (maximal-strength, measured by total weight lifted once) resulted in a greater number of submaximal repetitions (strength-endurance). Bottom line, the stronger you are, the more of that strength you can apply as muscular-endurance. SE training is placed after MS training in periodized plans for this reason. First build up maximal-strength, then convert it into strength-endurance. Don't train SE in isolation for too long without occasionally returning to MS to top off the source.

Power, power-endurance, and other strength-related subdomains are similar to SE, they rely on max-strength for optimal expression.

On the conditioning side:

> **Aerobic base >Specific Strength (Hills/elevation)/Anaerobic Capacity> Speed**

The aerobic system is trained throughout. Aerobic *base* training is a temporary initial phase that targets specific aspects of the aerobic system. The primary mode of cardiovascular training in this book is running, so I added specific strength work to the list, which consists of hill/elevation training. Speed work should become more concentrated and specific the closer you are to your event if applicable. In our world, there may be several different events within a given time period, so a more general approach can be taken.

All of the training in this program develops work capacity, but Peggy's Hills, the Strength-Endurance templates, Back-to-Backs, and two-a-days emphasize mixed modality work and building tolerance to volume.

You'll see the above order of operations loosely applied throughout Green Protocol. Use it as a guide when it's time to customize your own programming. Don't get OCD about it. It helps optimize results, but it's much more important to do the training than to nitpick the order.

SESSIONS

I - STRENGTH

Zulu/HT (Zulu)

Operator/Professional (Op/PRO, OP)

Operator/Daily Undulating Periodization (Op/DUP, OP)

Fighter (FT)

Strength-Endurance Training (SE)

II - CONDITIONING

Low Intensity Steady State Run (LSS)

400 Meter Repeats (400)

800 Meter Repeats (800)

Mile Repeats (MR)

Tempo Run (Tempo)

Fartlek (FK)

2/1 Run (2/1R)

Continuous Hill Run (Hill)

Vert Ladder (Hill)

Peggy's Hills (Peggy)

Hill Substitutes

Long Run (LR)

Weight Vest Run (WVR)

Ruck (Ruck)

Speed Ruck (S/Ruck)

III - DELOAD

STRENGTH

ZULU/HT

Zulu/HT is a hybrid mass/strength template and can be used anytime a focused hypertrophy phase is needed. Deceptively simple, it's a monster template that'll pack on muscle, increase strength, and improve work capacity. It focuses on four major compounds: Overhead Press, Squat, Bench Press, and Deadlift. Zulu also caters to operational athletes by incorporating regular pull-ups. Additional assistance work is also an option for those that are so inclined.

Zulu and it's variations were originally designed for tactical law enforcement (SWAT, ETF, TRU, etc.). Tactical LEOs often benefit from extra muscle and strength. Operations usually involve load bearing (HBA, breaching tools, shields) and there's a high likelihood of going hands-on with the bad guys. LE operations are relatively brief and rarely involve endurance-based movement over great distances. LEOs can usually get away with carrying more mass than their military counterparts.

When using Zulu/HT keep conditioning minimal. When you run a hypertrophy block the goal is hypertrophy, not improving your 2 mile time. Put that spare time and energy into more lifting: accessory work, extra sets, etc.

Week	Day 1	Day 2	Day 4	Day 5
1	OH 4 x 5 75% SQ 4 x 10 65% A 3-5x12 60%	DL 4 x 5 75% BP 4 x 10 65% B 3-5x12 60%	SQ 4 x 5 75% OH 4 x 10 65% A 3-5 x 12 60%	BP 4 x 5 75% DL 4 x 10 65% B 3-5x12 60%
2	OH 4 x 4 80% SQ 4 x 8 70% A 3-5x10 65%	DL 4 x 4 80% BP 4 x 8 70% B 3-5x10 65%	SQ 4 x 4 80% OH 4 x 8 70% A 3-5x10 65%	BP 4 x 4 80% DL 4 x 8 70% B 3-5x10 65%
3 Peak+ (optional)	OH 4 x 3 85%+ SQ 4 x 6 75% A 3-5x8 70%	DL 4 x 3 85%+ BP 4 x 6 75% B 3-5x8 70%	SQ 4 x 3 85%+ OH 4 x 6 75% A 3-5x8 70%	BP 4 x 3 85%+ DL 4 x 6 75% B 3-5x8 70%
SETS x REPS/ 1RM				

Standard Cluster	Assistance A	Assistance B
Overhead Press (OH) Squat (SQ) Bench Press (BP) Deadlift (DL)	Pull-Ups + 2-3 Accessories (optional)	Pull-Ups + 2-3 Accessories (optional)

ALTERNATE CLUSTERS

The Standard Cluster is best practice. Tested and proven, it builds strength and mass with extreme efficiency. That said, being an operational athlete gives you leeway because you're not training to compete in specific lifts. If desired, switch up some of the exercises or use variants. If you'd rather do front squats, do front squats. Incline bench instead of flat? Go for it.

ASSISTANCE WORK

Pull-Ups: If you're an operational athlete, include them for most or all sessions. If 4 times a week is too much, do 2-3 times. There are several ways to incorporate pull-ups. You can do bodyweight, weighted, or a mix of both. Do bodyweight pull-ups for percentage of max reps. Do weighted pull-ups using 1RM (include your bodyweight when calculating). Follow the heavy main lift rep/set/load scheme. Or do both. Cluster A can be weighted and Cluster B bodyweight. If you can't do a pull-up, use an appropriate substitute like assisted/band pull-ups, negatives, or partials. After you reach your first pull-up make the switch and do sets of 1 if necessary.

Assistance: In addition to pull-ups, you can include more assistance work. Pick 2-6 exercises and divide them between cluster A and B. Cluster A might be Barbell Rows and hanging leg raises, cluster B dips and reverse hypers. Follow the 'A' and 'B' rep/set scheme in the Zulu/HT table.

Don't overthink assistance work. The recommended programming percentages are primarily for the pull-ups. You can ditch them for the other exercises. You can go off feel and focus on the sets and reps instead. If you do use the prescribed percentages, use percentage of total reps for bodyweight work. If using weight, no need to get OCD with 1 rep maximums. Guesstimating is fine for assistance work. Aside from pull-ups, assistance is optional.

EXECUTION

Each session consists of two main lifts + pull-ups + optional assistance work.

Perform the main lifts first.

4 sets is the standard recommendation. You can do 3-5 if/when you have more or less time/energy.

Percentage of Total Reps can be used for bodyweight exercises like pull-ups or dips. If you can do a maximum of 10 pull-ups, and it's 65% week, do sets of 6 or 7. Round up or down as desired.

Rest for approximately 2-5 minutes between sets, or longer if needed. It's better to be rested enough to complete all reps than to jump into a new set too quickly and fail to finish.

PEAKING

During Week 3 peaking techniques can be used. This is optional. Pick one of the following and apply it to the heavy lift of the session:

PEAKING: Complete only 1 work set of 3 reps at 85%. After that keep adding a little weight to the bar and rep out singles, doubles, triples etc. See how far you can go.

AMRAP: As Many Reps As Possible. On the last set don't stop at 4 reps. Keep going see how many you can do.

AMSAP: As Many Sets As Possible. Don't stop at 4 sets. Keep going for as long as you like.

PROGRESSION

Add approximately 5-10lbs to 1 Rep Maximums every 3-6 weeks.

5lbs to Upper Body Lifts

5-10lbs to Lower Body Lifts

Retest Pull-Ups or add 2-3 reps to maximums

Recalculate/Execute

Test your pull-ups/other bodyweight exercises and use the new maximums. If you're stalling on pull-ups/other bodyweight, force progression by adding 2-3 reps to your maximums and recalculating.

OPERATOR/PRO

AKA Primary/Secondary. This template exemplifies one of our driving principles at TB – 'simplicity is the ultimate sophistication'. If you've squeezed everything you can out of standard Operator, this template is the next logical step. It's ideal for lifters that are venturing into intermediate/advanced territory with a need for sharper stimulus balanced with a manageable session, alongside heavy conditioning. It's also a lot of fun.

Week	Day 1	Day 3	Day 5
1	BENCH: 2-3RM SQ 3-5 x 5 65% DL 3-5 x 5 65%	SQUAT: 2-3RM BP 3-5 x 5 65% DL 3-5 x 5 65%	DEADLIFT: 2-3RM BP 3-5 x 5 65% SQ 3-5 x 5 65%
2	BENCH: 2-3RM SQ 3-5 x 5 70% DL 3-5 x 5 70%	SQUAT: 2-3RM BP 3-5 x 5 70% DL 3-5 x 5 70%	DEADLIFT: 2-3RM BP 3-5 x 5 70% SQ 3-5 x 5 70%
3 Peak Week	BENCH: Peak SQ 3-5 x 5 75% DL 3-5 x 5 75%	SQUAT: Peak BP 3-5 x 5 75% DL 3-5 x 5 75%	DEADLIFT: Peak BP 3-5 x 5 75% SQ 3-5 x 5 75%
Sets x Reps			

The first lift of the session is the primary. Work your way up to a 2 or 3 rep max. I'm not going to prescribe exact numbers, but ballpark 3-5 sets of 2-5 reps with or without your warm-ups. More or less as needed. It'll depend on you and how much volume you want to incorporate. Hit a nice heavy double or triple, and you're done. The number you reach might vary on any given day based on your level of fatigue. Some days you'll be able to go heavier, other days not. This is a form of automatic self-regulation, a feature, not a bug. I can already see the OCD minds starting to spin trying to calculate a 2-3RM based on a 1RM to create a pre-planned, ultraprecise, NORAD accurate weight to work up to. Stop. Work up to a 2-3 rep maximum *for that session*. It may or may not always be in line with your tested 1 rep maximum. If you're not comfortable with this kind of ambiguity use standard Operator or Op/DUP instead until you have a little more experience under your belt.

The secondary lifts are performed with lighter weight. The secondaries have a very important role, they add volume and increase frequency. Volume and frequency increase strength and hypertrophy. The secondaries allow intermediate/advanced lifters to reap the benefits of frequency and volume while keeping individual sessions manageable, and compatible with heavier conditioning. You get to focus on the main lift, while greasing the groove with the secondaries. ('Greasing the groove' is a term introduced by renowned strength and kettlebell coach Pavel Tsatsouline. Do some google-fu to learn more.)

SECONDARIES/ADJUSTING LOAD

Everything is relative. Depending on how experienced you are, 65% RM can be 30lbs or 300lbs. If you're a veteran lifter with respectable maximums, feel free to use a training max for the secondary lifts if the load and volume exceed what you can manage in a single session.

CLUSTER

The recommended cluster is the Bench Press, Squat, and Trapbar Deadlift. Alternatives can be used, such as the Front Squat, Incline Bench, Sumo, etc.

PULL-UP FINISHER/ASSISTANCE WORK

Optional if you're a civilian or recreational trainee but strongly recommendded for operational athletes. Do 3-5 sets of weighted or bodyweight pull-ups at the end of each session. Use Secondary programming. Percentage of total reps for bodyweight, percentage of 1 rep max for weighted (include your bodyweight when calculating 1RM).

Assistance work focusing on ab/core, grip, and neck training can be added.

LESS DEADLIFTING

Deadlifts can be tricky for some people. More so if they're already fairly strong and/or very active. It doesn't take much to tweak or stress the back - one careless DL rep when you're tired or unfocused, and you might be out of the game for a while. For many, frequent or volume DL sessions also exact a high recovery cost. If you respond to or prefer less frequent deadlifting, you can do them once a week on their designated day. Or just do one work set on non-primary days to pattern the movement and improve that neuromuscular connection. The great thing about DLs is that they don't need a ton of attention, especially when you're also squatting three times a week. One session a week is the sweet spot for many. At the end of the day, you're not training to be a better at deadlifts, you're training for combat fitness. Big picture.

INCREASED HYPERTROPHY

In the standard model the secondaries are kept light & tight at five reps. This is the sweet spot for high speed operators that do a lot of hardcore conditioning. That said, it can be programmed for increased mass and used as needed. You're going to tweak the **secondary** programming by increasing the reps like this:

Week 1: 3-5 sets x 10 reps
Week 2: 3-5 sets x 8 reps
Week 3: 3-5 sets x 6 reps

A very simple adjustment but watch what it does for your muscle mass.

WEEK 3/ PEAK WEEK

Programming changes slightly come Week 3. Pick one of the following options and apply it to the primary lift:

PEAKING: Work up to your double or triple. After that keep adding a little weight to the bar and rep out singles. See how heavy you can go. This can also serve as 1RM testing to get a snapshot of your progress.

AMSAP: As Many Sets As Possible. Work up to your double or triple. Then do as many sets as possible or as many as you like.

EXECUTION

Rest for approximately 2-5 minutes between sets or longer as needed.

Best practice is to perform the primary lift first while you're fresh, but that's not mandatory.

Grease the groove, build volume, and add frequency with the secondary lifts.

Perform the pull-up finisher at the end of the session. If using bodyweight, apply the prescribed percentages to your maximum number of reps. For example, if you max out at 10 pull-ups, week 1 would be 3-5 sets of 6 or 7 pull-ups (65% of 10 is 6.5). Round up or down.

If using weighted pull-ups, include your bodyweight when calculating 1RM.

PROGRESSION

Add approximately 5-10lbs to 1 Rep Maximums every 3-6 weeks.

5lbs to Upper Body Lifts

10lbs to Lower Body Lifts

Retest Pull-Ups or add 2-3 reps to maximums

Recalculate

If you're struggling with one or more lift, one of the best progression strategies is to do nothing. Use the same numbers for the upcoming block. Give yourself time to grow into the weight and own it.

OPERATOR/DUP

The Daily Undulating Periodization version of Operator template. Each session trains multiple domains concurrently; maximal-strength, hypertrophy, and speed/power.

The Op/DUP standard cluster consists of the bench press, squat, and trapbar deadlift. Plyometric variants can be used for the speed/power component of the session. Pull-ups are incorporated as a finisher, adding a little bit of unofficial muscular-endurance and specific strength for those that need it.

SESSION BREAKDOWN

Lift #1 Maximal-Strength

Lift #2 Hypertrophy

Lift #3 Power/Speed

Finisher: Pull-Ups (specific strength/muscular endurance)

The maximal-strength lift of the session is performed using heavy loads/low reps.

The hypertrophy lift is performed with medium to heavy loads. We're using the lower end of the hypertrophy rep range and higher end of load to maximize strength and dense muscle mass. Staying on the heavier/lower rep end of the hypertrophy spectrum aligns with the needs of combat fitness in this context. Op/DUP is usually used in the presence of increased conditioning, more so than hypertrophy leaning templates like Zulu/HT.

The speed/power lift is performed dynamically with light loads (50-60%RM) and low reps (sets of 2-3 reps). Speed of execution is the name of the game. Move submaximal load at maximum velocity. Speed and explosiveness are applied during the concentric portion of the exercise. This part of the session has several objectives. It improves force output, speed, and overall athleticism. It adds weekly frequency and volume for each lift/movement. It regulates session intensity – the power/speed exercise is relatively easy which keeps the overall workload of the session manageable. You'll have the option to substitute similar kind power-centric exercises such as plyometric push-ups or squat jumps in place of the traditional lifts.

The session concludes with specific strength/muscular-endurance in the form of a pull-up finisher. Pull-Ups have a special place in the Tactical Barbell system. They're generally included in some way shape or form during most phases of Green Protocol. Pull-Ups provide exceptional strength benefits, require minimal recovery, and are directly applicable to combat fitness (caving ladders, obstacle courses, rappelling/climbing etc.). They're almost always found in periodic or entry level fitness tests. They're usually the most challenging exercise in these tests, therefore always staying on top of them ensures you can hit a PFT at anytime with minimal disruption to your regular training. During Op/DUP, pull-ups can be performed weighted or bodyweight.

Week	Day 1	Day 3	Day 5
1	BP 3-5 x 5 75% SQ 3-4 x 8 70% DL 3-5 x 2-3 50% PU 3-5 x 50%	SQ 3-5 x 5 75% DL 3-4 x 8 70% BP 3-5 x 2-3 50% PU 3-5 x 50%	DL 3-5 x 5 75% BP 3-4 x 8 70% SQ 3-5 x 2-3 50% PU 3-5 x 50%
2	BP 3-5 x 4 80% SQ 3-4 x 6 75% DL 3-5 x 2-3 55% PU 3-5 x 60%	SQ 3-5 x 4 80% DL 3-4 x 6 75% BP 3-5 x 2-3 55% PU 3-5 x 60%	DL 3-5 x 4 80% BP 3-4 x 6 75% SQ 3-5 x 2-3 55% PU 3-5 x 60%
3	BP 3 x 3 85% SQ 3-4 x 4 80% DL 3-5 x 2-3 60% PU 3-5 x 70%	SQ 3 x 3 85% DL 3-4 x 4 80% BP 3-5 x 2-3 60% PU 3-5 x 70%	DL 3 x 3 85% BP 3-4 x 4 80% SQ 3-5 x 2-3 60% PU 3-5 x 70%
Sets x Reps			

STANDARD CLUSTER

Bench Press (BP)

Squat (SQ)

Trapbar Deadlift (DL)

Pull-Ups (PU)

Plyometric variants can be used for the dynamic exercise (see below)

ALTERNATE CLUSTERS

The standard cluster is best practice, but you can customize or create your own if desired. Rule of thumb is to include a press, a pull, and legs. For example, the Front Squat or Incline Bench can be subbed in for Squat or Bench.

Pull-ups can be performed weighted. Include bodyweight when calculating 1RM and follow the rep/set/load scheme for either the max-strength or hypertrophy lift.

Regarding the **Deadlift**. I recommend the trapbar or sumo for both Op/PRO and Op/DUP blocks. The trapbar in particular is very compatible with high volume conditioning. Heavy conventional DLs exact a high price in terms of recovery and can impact your running/elevation training. Conventional also places more direct pressure on the lumbar/lower back region. If your heart's set on conventional, do conventional, but monitor it's effects on your conditioning sessions.

Alternate Dynamic Movements. Instead of using the bench, squat, and deadlift for the speed lift, sub in similar movements that emphasize power and explosiveness. For example, plyometric push-ups instead of the bench press, box jumps or squat jumps for the squat, and plyometric pull-ups for deadlifts. Bands fit here as well.

Sample: Op/DUP + Alternate Power/Speed Movements		
BP	SQ	DL
SQ	DL	BP
Plyometric Pull-Ups	*Plyometric Push-Ups*	*Box Jumps*
Finisher: Pull-Ups	Finisher: Pull-Ups	Finisher: Pull-Ups

NO PULL-UPS?

I've spent a bunch of time extolling the virtues of pull-ups, now I'm going to do an about-face and let you opt out. In *some* cases, you may not need to include pull-up finishers in Op/DUP or Op/PRO:

You already have a solid pull-up foundation and don't need much work to keep your numbers up. You're fine with just touching them up before PFT or as needed.

You're a civilian or pull-ups aren't a high value/tested exercise for your role.

You're going to get a chance to train pull-ups full bore during Strength-Endurance (SE) blocks and Fighter template. The pull-ups during the SE & Fighter portions of this program might be more than enough for your situation. If so, you can hold off until then.

If you fall into any of the above categories, you can drop the pull-ups completely, sprinkle them in when you feel like it, or save them for SE and Fighter blocks. This lets you focus on the main lifts and gives you a tighter Op/DUP or PRO session. If you're preparing for (or in) an operational role and struggle to hit 10 pull-ups at any given time, ignore this, keep them in your cluster.

EXECUTION

The first lift of the session emphasizes maximal-strength, the second hypertrophy, and the third speed/power.

Best practice is to perform the maximal-strength and hypertrophy lifts first, and the speed/power exercise last.

Perform the power exercise with maximum speed and explosiveness during the concentric portion of the movement. Stay in control and maintain excellent form.

Perform the pull-up finisher at the very end of the session. Apply the prescribed percentages to your maximum number of reps. For example, if you max out at 10 pull-ups, week 1 would be 3-5 sets of 5 pull-ups (50% of 10 is 5). Round up or down.

If using weighted pull-ups, the maximal-strength or hypertrophy loading pattern can be used. Include your bodyweight when calculating 1RM.

A note on waviness. Sessions give you a range such as 3-5 sets. Trainees have different approaches or methods for dealing with this. Some use a higher set range during the early weeks to get more volume in while the work is light, others might want to focus on a particular domain or weak lift - they maximize sets for the target exercise while minimizing sets for lower priority exercises. These are all excellent practices. Another approach is to use it as a way to self-regulate individual sessions. Don't plan out the number of sets beforehand. When you're tired, use the lower end or minimums. On days you're not, go higher. Sometimes it comes down to logistics. If strapped for time, do the minimum on some or all of the exercises. If you have more time than usual, do the maximum. Another approach to consider.

PROGRESSION

Add approximately 5-10lbs to 1 Rep Maximums every 3-6 weeks.

5lbs to Upper Body Lifts

10lbs to Lower Body Lifts

Retest Pull-Ups or add 2-3 reps to maximums

Recalculate

If you're struggling with one or more lift, one of the best progression strategies is to do nothing. Use the same numbers for the upcoming block. Give yourself time to grow into the weight and own it.

FIGHTER

A favorite among MMA athletes, ultra runners, and special operations personnel, Fighter is the ultimate high speed/low drag two day template. It thrives alongside heavy conditioning and specialized skill work. Fighter leverages frequency to optimize progress. Each major lift is performed twice a week, which makes it much more effective than many traditional two day templates. Don't let the minimalist look fool you – you can gain significant strength with this template.

Fighter is generally used in the presence of high volume conditioning or endurance training, so keep your cluster streamlined/minimal. It's not the time to be adding a bunch of assistance work or trying to hit all 115 planes of vertical and horizontal movement. Give most of your love to your conditioning sessions and let strength training to take on a supporting role. You'll progress and get stronger, but at a slower pace so you can pay the endurance bills. You're a hybrid athlete now. Be agile and use the principles of prioritization to your advantage.

WEEK	DAY 1	DAY 4
1	OP 3-5 x 5 75% FS 3-5 x 5 75% WP 3-5 x 5 75%	OP 3-5 x 5 75% FS 3-5 x 5 75% WP 3-5 x 5 75%
2	OP 3-5 x 4 80% FS 3-5 x 4 80% WP 3-5 x 4 80%	OP 3-5 x 4 80% FS 3-5 x 4 80% WP 3-5 x 4 80%
3	OP 3-5 x 3 85% FS 3-5 x 3 85% WP 3-5 x 3 85%	OP 3-5 x 3 85% FS 3-5 x 3 85% WP 3-5 x 3 85%
Sets x Reps		

STANDARD CLUSTER

Overhead Press (OP)

Front Squat (FS)

Weighted Pull-Up (WP)*

*Bodyweight pull-ups can be used.

ALTERNATE CLUSTERS

Alternate exercises can be used such as the bench press, squat, weighted push-ups, weighted dips, weighted single leg squats, etc. Rule of thumb is to include a press, a pull, and a leg movement.

Deadlifts can be added to the standard cluster if desired. 1-3 sets once or twice a week is fine. The trapbar or sumo variation is recommended. Proceed with caution. One deadlift session per week is usually enough.

Pull-Ups are performed every session. Weighted is best practice for this template, but bodyweight can be used.

Weighted: Include your bodyweight when calculating 1 rep maximum. If sessions call for you to use bodyweight or less – use the percentage of max reps instead (see below) until you reach a session that puts you over. It's not uncommon for those new to WPs to start out week 1 using nothing but bodyweight and switching to weighted sometime during week 2 or even 3. It may take even longer.

Bodyweight: Apply the prescribed percentages to your maximum number of reps instead. For example, if your maximum is 8 pull-ups, week 1 would be 3-5 sets of 6 (75% of 8 is 6). This also applies to you if you're doing weighted pull-ups but haven't reached a load that requires you to add external weight yet. Do them using percentage of total reps until you reach a session that puts you over your bodyweight.

EXECUTION

Rest for approximately 2-5 minutes between sets, or longer if needed. Be rested enough to complete all reps of each set.

Exercises can be performed in any order or even circuit style.

PROGRESSION

Add 2.5-10lbs to 1 Rep Maximums every 3-6 weeks.

2.5-5lbs to upper body exercises

10lbs to lower body exercises

Recalculate

STRENGTH-ENDURANCE TRAINING

Maximal-strength (MS) is the ability to generate force. Strength-Endurance (SE) aka muscular-endurance is the ability to apply that force repeatedly over a period of time. Structured SE training is one way to directly improve muscular-endurance.

SE programming in Green Protocol is a variation on existing Tactical Barbell Strength-Endurance templates. There are two models, a 2 and 3 day. Each block is three weeks in length, plus a fourth deload week. Exercises can be done weight-less or with a bit of resistance in the form of a weight vest, light barbells, dumbbells, kettlebells, bands, etc.

STEP 1 – CREATE AN EXERCISE CLUSTER

Pick 3-5 exercises. Your cluster should consist of movements typically associated with the military/law enforcement or specific events you're preparing for. Push-ups, pull-ups, and abs/core are usually a common theme. Use the same exercise cluster for the entire block.

SAMPLE CLUSTERS			
Push-Ups	Burpees	Kettlebell Swings	H/Release Push-Up
Pull-Ups	Pull-Ups	Push-Ups	KB Sumo Deadlift
Single Leg Squats	Goblet Squats	Pull-Ups	KB Push Press
Ab Roller	Crunches	Step Ups	Leg Tuck
		Hanging Leg raise	

INCORPORATE A WEIGHT VEST

If you're training for a more advanced unit or role, consider using a weight vest for your bodyweight movements. Don't go too heavy. Going too heavy takes you out of that strength-endurance sweet spot and starts turning your session into a maximal-strength workout. 5-10lbs is sufficient to start, with the upper range being for experienced trainees with a solid SE foundation. The idea is to add a little bit of drag to enhance results without venturing into maximal-strength territory. If your cluster contains exercises that interfere with the vest (like crunches or leg tucks) save them for last and take it off prior to execution. A weight vest can change the dynamic of an exercise. For example, Step-Ups are decent on their own, but adding weight makes them more applicable to load bearing/combat fitness.

STEP 2 – ESTABLISH STARTING NUMBERS

Take a day or two and test the maximum number of reps you can do for each exercise in your cluster. No need to be OCD, get close enough.

STEP 3 – EXECUTE 2 OR 3 DAY TEMPLATE

During Foundation the templates are chosen for you. Come Continuation, you get to choose.

SE / 2 DAY		
Week	Session 1	Session 2
1	4-5 x 50%	4-5 x 50%
2	4-5 x 60%	4-5 x 60%
3	4-5 x 70%	4-5 x 70%
4 Deload	2 x 30%	2 x 30%

SE / 3 DAY			
Week	Session 1	Session 2	Session 3
1	3-5 x 50%	3-5 x 50%	3 x 90%
2	3-5 x 60%	3-5 x 60%	3 x 90%
3	3-5 x 70%	3-5 x 70%	3 x 90%
4 Deload	2 x 30%	2 x 30%	Rest for Retest

EXECUTION

The template is laid out as Sets or Circuits x Percentage of Maximum Reps. If your maximum number of push-ups is 80, week 1 would be sets of 40(50% of 80 is 40). Round up or down as required.

All exercises in the cluster are performed each session.

SE can be performed circuit-style or one exercise at a time.

Take 1-2 minutes of rest between sets or less.

Rest for 3-5 minutes between circuits or exercises.

When you fail to complete a set, take a 30 second break and squeeze out mini-sets of 1-5 reps. Repeat until finished.

Circuit training is best practice. Move from one exercise to another with minimal rest. If your weight vest interferes with a particular exercise, leave the exercise out and do it at the end of the circuit. Rest for 3-5 minutes between circuits.

Circuit training isn't always possible due to gym logistics, equipment availability, tying up several stations at once etc. The next best thing is to stack two or more exercises together and alternate between them. Take 1-2 minutes between sets and 3-5 minutes between exercise pairs. Try and keep the rest minimal between sets.

If circuit training or stacking aren't an option, do one exercise at a time. Rest for 1-2 minutes or less between sets and 3-5 minutes between exercises.

SE training is messy. You're going to be all over the place and won't always stay within the prescribed rest intervals. For exercises like pull-ups, you might be extending that rest even more. At the end of the day, the objective is to complete all the prescribed reps of the session, without being **fully** rested. Minimizing the rest interval is a secondary objective, something to keep in the back of your mind while training. You don't need to pull out a stopwatch and chart the progression of micro-seconds between sessions over the block. Find a balance between completing most reps of a set before failure, and minimal rest.

STEP 4 – DELOAD & RETEST

Take a break. Drop SE training completely if your joints and tendons are mad at you. Or do 20-30% max reps and half the prescribed circuits. Take the weight vest off. Retest over the last couple days of the week to establish new starting numbers. If there's no change to your numbers force progression by adding 5-10 reps to the stalled exercise. For example, if you started the block being able to do 80 push-ups, and still can't do more than 80 push-ups by the end of it, make your new max 90. Use fewer reps to progress the challenging exercises like pull-ups.

You can also change or adjust your cluster at this point if desired. I recommend sticking with the same cluster for several blocks for maximum benefit, but it's not mandatory, especially if you're looking for general overall SE development rather than specific exercise or movement based improvement.

CONDITIONING

LOW INTENSITY STEADY STATE RUN

'You will come to your peak slower than many others and you will be running last when they are running first. But when it is really important to be running first, you will be passing them.'

Arthur Lydiard

Easy, steady-state jogging. Sometimes referred to as Zone 2. Irreplaceable for the endurance-based operator. LSS lays an aerobic foundation and increases overall work capacity. It allows for sustainable higher weekly mileage and is one of the best ways to directly target the aerobic system. It's also my sneaky way of slipping in a recovery day (with benefits) between harder sessions.

LSS is prescribed in minutes or miles.

LSS 30-60 = Jog for 30 to 60 minutes.

Or:

LSS 5 = Jog for five miles

Each template will specify which prescription is being used.

Jog at an easy pace for the prescribed distance or time. Keep heartrate *roughly* in the aerobic zone, somewhere between 120-150 beats per minute. If you don't have a heartrate monitor, use the talk-test. Jog slowly enough to have a conversation with your imaginary friend. Be able to speak in paragraphs. Don't lose sleep over it. Heartrate perimeters are provided to give you an idea of what 'slow' and 'easy' should feel like for you. The more out of shape you are (aerobically), the slower that's likely going to be.

For Capacity, and ONLY Capacity, stick to flat roads or flat trails. You're going to use Capacity to teach your body what easy feels like. This will be your 4 out of 10 pace, or RPE 4 (Rate of Perceived Exertion).

AFTER CAPACITY

For all other templates and phases LSS is done offroad/on trails. Drop the heartrate monitor and go by feel or RPE. Jog at a 4-5 out of 10. Think back to your LSS during Capacity if you can't remember what slow & easy feels like. You can occasionally look at your monitor to ensure you're not wildly off base, but don't slavishly adhere to it.

The best practice is to jog on offroad trails with a bit of elevation. The ideal route has some gently rolling terrain and maybe one or two steeper inclines. The name of the game is still easy and steady. Don't do speed intervals. Don't sprint up the hills. Don't push your pace on the flats. Apply a low level of effort but understand the terrain will dictate your heartrate at times. When the hills are steep, stop jogging and hike them. When they're not, jog over them. General rule of thumb is if you can see over the incline keep jogging, if you can't, hike it and continue jogging on the downslope. Be seamless and smooth with your transitions from jogging to hiking. When you hike, hike with purpose. Don't stroll up the hill smelling the flowers.

By incorporating elevation in LSS, you get the aerobic benefit, specific-strength, and muscular-endurance training. Additionally, controlling your level of effort over irregular terrain will teach you to conserve energy, establish a rhythm, and maintain momentum. Skills which are going to be invaluable come selection or ops. Over time, you'll be able to jog more of the inclines while staying in the aerobic zone. When you can stay low-effort/aerobic, and relatively fast for the majority of a hilly run, regardless of ascent/descent, you're winning.

Aside from the aerobic and strength benefits, the 'ebb and flow' approach carries over to rucking. It'll teach you how to maintain speed while minimizing fatigue. Pick up the pace when it's flat, hike the inclines in a more conservative fashion. The harsh reality is if you're preparing for a high-end ruck intensive selection/school, you might need to ruck-run to meet some of your timings. If you happen to find yourself in such a situation, you can apply ebb and flow - jog the flats, power-hike the inclines.

LSS is effective partly because it trains the aerobic system mostly in isolation. You're forcing yourself to go slowly enough to stay in the aerobic zone, so the other energy systems don't kick in. Contrast that with something like 400M Repeats where the anerobic system steps in and takes over a portion of the work. By controlling your level of effort, the aerobic system ends up doing most of the work by itself which results in a more concentrated training effect.

LSS can feel abnormally slow in the beginning. Possibly a few geriatric walkers might even pass you. How it plays out is you might need to slow down at first to stay in the zone. Maybe 10-15 minute miles or even slower. Over time, as your aerobic system improves, your pace will increase at the same level of effort. Now you're running 8 or 9 minute miles at roughly the same heartrate or perceived effort. Eventually, what was once your tempo pace becomes your relaxed aerobic pace, a pace you can maintain forever. Consider the benefits of that.

A truly unique training tool, LSS can facilitate recovery after harder workouts while simultaneously improving your cardiovascular fitness. You're recovering and getting better at the same time. In Green Protocol LSS runs double as active recovery days and act as a bridge between harder sessions.

LSS isn't the ONLY way to train the aerobic system or endurance. Different forms of training improve different aspects. LSS is just one angle of attack, a single piece of the puzzle. Speedwork and interval training improve the aerobic system. Hill sessions improve the aerobic system. You need all the pieces to optimize performance, not just one, not just the other.

CUSTOMIZING LSS

If you're using Green Protocol for Military/Law Enforcement/Fire, the majority of your LSS work should be in the form of running. Modes like cycling or swimming are too efficient. They don't have the same effect as locomoting your body without assistance. Treadmill running is a step up from cycling or swimming, but not as effective as propelling yourself over real ground. You can use these other forms of LSS to supplement your training, but they shouldn't be the norm. Use them occasionally to pull back from running if overuse issues like tendonitis loom.

If you're a civvy/recreational trainee, other modalities can be used as desired – cycling, swimming, jump rope, shadow boxing, step-ups, etc. The key is to ensure the activity you choose allows you to keep your heartrate or level of effort within the prescribed zone for the duration of the session. Remember, *low-intensity, steady state*.

LSS will help you keep weekly mileage high without getting burnt out. It also does double duty as an active recovery session. If you go too fast, you'll lose out on the benefits and potentially wear yourself out for future training. Endurance is a long game. You have to gently build up a significant amount of volume while dodging overuse injury and burnout. LSS makes that possible – if you're doing it right. Let LSS do the job of LSS. Let other sessions deal with speed and other aspects of running. If at any point you feel like you're pushing too hard, stop. Walk for a couple minutes, reset, and recommit yourself to a relaxed low effort pace.

400 METER REPEATS

A favorite among powerhouse runners such as Emil Zatopek and Eliud Kipchoge, 400 Meter Repeats will turn you into a speed demon.

400Ms are prescribed using rounds in this format:

400/10

Translation: Perform 10 rounds.

Run 400 meters at your fastest sustainable pace.

Jog or walk 400 meters at a recovery pace.

Repeat.

One round includes both the 400 work/rest portions. Beginners can walk the recovery lap; others should jog it.

These are not the same as the 600M Resets found in Tactical Barbell II. Resets are performed at maximum speed after maximum rest, with the objective of extending the duration of maximum output. 400M Repeats are done at a fast pace, but one that can be maintained for the duration of the session. In other words, go fast but pace yourself.

800 METER REPEATS

800M Repeats are prescribed using rounds in this format:

800/2-4

Translation: Perform 2-4 rounds.

Run 800 meters at your fastest sustainable pace.

Walk for 3-5 minutes or jog for 800 meters at a recovery pace.

Repeat

800M Repeats are done at a fast pace, but one that can be maintained for the duration of the session. Go fast, but pace yourself.

MILE REPEATS

Mile Repeats build speed, speed-endurance, and aerobic capacity. They're excellent for working on timed runs such as the 1.5, 2 mile, and others typically found in PFTs, selection, and annual qualifications. Mile Repeats are prescribed in rounds:

MR 3 = 3 x Mile Repeats

Warm-up Jog x 10-15 minutes

Run 1 Mile at Maximum Sustainable Effort

Jog or Walk for 1/2 Duration of 1 Mile Time

Repeat for Prescribed # of Rounds

Run your work mile at maximum speed, but a speed you can maintain. Note how long it takes and rest for approximately half that time. For example, if it takes you 8 minutes to complete the mile, jog or walk at a recovery pace for 4 minutes. Round up or down, don't get OCD and calculate half minutes or seconds.

Additionally, pace can be used to prepare for specific distances and events. For example, choose a benchmark like the 1.5 mile or 2 mile run. The 1.5 is a common event found all over the military/police world in various tests and selections. Set a target time. For operational athletes I recommend working toward a 9 minute 1.5 mile or faster. Adjust accordingly depending on the role. Let's say you currently run the 1.5 in 12 minutes. That puts you at a pace of roughly 8 minutes per mile. To get to a 9 minute 1.5 you'll need to achieve a pace of 6 minutes per mile. When you do your Mile Repeats, work on increasing your speed by 15-30 second increments. Your first goal post might be a 7:30 min/mile. Try to keep your Repeats at roughly 7:30 or under. I say roughly because it can be challenging to maintain an exact pace within seconds indefinitely. Slight variations in terrain or speed can easily throw your pace off. When you can comfortably hold a 7:30ish pace, set your next objective: try to hit a 7 minute mile or under... and so on. Use smaller or larger increments (15 seconds etc.) as needed.

Keep in mind it'll take time to meet your new pacing objectives. It won't happen overnight. Also, don't get discouraged if you slow down drastically after the first round. Subsequent repeats are usually harder due to fatigue. You will improve over time. It's a great feeling going from being barely able to complete your third repeat to holding a steady quick pace for five or six of them.

Mile Repeats are great at revealing deficiencies in your diet. If you're restricting carbs don't be surprised if you feel like you've been hit by a truck after the second or third round. For longer MR sessions, I suggest packing some quick acting sugar like GU or Gatorade.

Mile Repeats are one part of a whole. All the sessions (LSS, Tempo, strength training) contribute to overall conditioning, run times, and performance. Don't make the mistake of just doing Mile Repeats to cram before a 1.5 Mile test. You need speed *and* staying power. Not just one, not just the other.

TEMPO RUN

A Tempo Run is a fast run done at a sustainable pace. Tempo Runs are prescribed in miles using this format:

Tempo 3 = Tempo Run x 3 Miles

Warmup Jog 1 Mile

Tempo Run 3 Miles

Cooldown Jog 1 Mile

All Tempo Runs begin and end with a one mile warmup/cool-down jog. Tempo 3 ends up being 5 miles in total. Do the warmup/cooldown at LSS pace or slower. Aside from being used to warm-up/cooldown, the extra mileage adds to overall weekly running volume. Overall weekly mileage is a contributing factor to endurance based conditioning.

Run at a 'comfortably hard' pace for the tempo portion. RPE is a preferred method. On a scale of 1-10, with your LSS pace being a 4-5 and your 1.5 mile race pace being a 10, a tempo run should be around 7-8. You should be able to blurt out brief phrases. If you can hold a conversation, you're going too slow. It'll end up being somewhere around 85%-90% of max heartrate. Pace can also be used. See 'Mile Repeats' for using pace.

FARTLEK

The Fartlek is essentially a Long Run with some speedwork thrown in. It's best done on a trail/offroad.

Jog at an easy LSS pace for 3-5 minutes.

Sprint for 10-60 seconds.

Repeat for the remainder of the run.

Jog for 10-15 minutes before doing the first sprint interval of the workout.

Vary the duration of your sprints. When using the lower end of the range (10-15 seconds) sprint at maximal or near-maximal effort. Adjust and manage the intensity for the longer intervals. This helps you develop and maintain speed for different distances and durations. Approach the Fartlek with a sense of play. If you come across hills that you want to sprint, then sprint. You can also use other natural landmarks instead of time to plan your intervals, i.e. sprint to the curve in the trail up ahead, or sprint up to the fourth tree on the right, etc.

Jog at a nice easy pace for the 3-5 minute recovery interval. You should be somewhat settled and relaxed before each high intensity effort. Extend the rest period if needed.

Fartlek sessions are prescribed using distance or duration.

2/1 RUN

The 2/1 is a short/high intensity interval run. The recovery portion is limited to two minutes so that you're never fully rested for the work intervals. The 2/1 is prescribed in minutes:

2/1R 30 = 30 Minutes

Jog for 2 minutes.

Run fast for 1 minute.

Repeat for the prescribed duration.

Ramp up the intensity of the work portion to a maximal or near maximal effort. Use the two minute jog to recover. Keep it brief. 2/1Rs are done for 20-30 minutes tops. Focus on quality and speed over duration. Anything longer than 20-30 minutes and intensity starts to deteriorate. Work on running a faster interval as opposed to stretching the session past 30 minutes.

The 2/1 is excellent for getting in quality speedwork when you're short on time or forced to use the treadmill. It makes for a great little 20 minute finisher after a lifting session. 2/1 programming can be applied to other modes of conditioning like cycling, rowing, and heavy bag work.

CONTINUOUS HILL RUN

The Continuous Hill Run is a powerful endurance and general conditioning tool. It'll beef up your quads, build massive amounts of muscular-endurance, and take your stamina to new levels.

Find a moderately steep hill or slope that gives you around 10-30 minutes of uphill jogging time. Think roads that wind around mountains or trails with longer stretches of constant incline. Your route should be roughly 80% runnable but if you have to stop and hike some of the steeper portions that's okay. Make do with what you have, it doesn't have to be perfect.

CHR = 30-120 Minutes (ascent time)

CHRs are done for 30 to 120 minutes of *uphill* time. The downhill portion doesn't count toward session time. Do more reps to reach total ascent time if using a shorter hill. There is no heartrate component or restriction. Listen to your body and self-regulate. On days you're beat up or short on time use the middle or lower end of the range. On days you have a little more pep go long. Pick a duration that makes sense for your goals. 120 minute sessions are usually reserved for very challenging selections, schools, or events. Most will be fine with 30-60 minutes.

Jog up the hill continuously at a relaxed sustainable pace. Stay loose. When you reach the top, jog or walk back down. Repeat for the prescribed duration. If you're out of shape you might not get far before having to walk. Not a big deal. Continue power-hiking (striding up the hill with purpose) until you're ready to break into a jog again. You can also use a 10/10 or 20/20 method to break up the ascent – walk for 10 or 20 paces, jog for 10 or 20 paces, repeat. Don't feel bad if you spend most of the time hiking at first – whether hiking or jogging, uphill movement is an extremely effective tool in and of itself for the military athlete. Over time you'll get farther up the hill before having to walk, and eventually you'll run the entire thing. As you get fitter, work on pushing the pace.

The downhill is almost as important and comes with it's own benefits. It'll condition your quads, knees, and stabilizers to take a beating from different angles. Take it slow until you get used to it. Do a mix of walking and jogging. You don't need much downhill training to benefit.

If you're in a selection or school situation, and rucking or running a timed route with elevation, you may need to maximize your speed on the descents to make up for time lost on the climbs. If you're not used to it, excessive downhill movement can quickly fatigue your muscles and supporting structures. Last thing you want is to slip and fall due to a lack of specific conditioning and loss of form. Incorporating purposeful downhill training will prepare you and give you an edge.

VERT LADDER

This one's great for building uphill running ability at various speeds. Find a moderate to steep hill or incline.

Run uphill x 1 minute/downhill recovery jog
Run uphill x 2 minutes/downhill recovery jog
Run uphill x 3 minutes/downhill recovery jog
Run uphill x 4 minutes/downhill recovery jog
Run uphill x 5 minutes/downhill recovery jog
Run uphill x 4 minutes/downhill recovery jog
….work your way back down the ladder to 1 minute.

This one lets you play with a variety of different climbing speeds. Go fast on the shorter ascents. Adjust and go slower on the longer. Go higher or lower than 5 minutes as needed.

PEGGY'S HILLS

Pegasus Hills is a brutally effective work capacity session: simple, low-tech, a cyborg-builder. Use it to prepare for challenging schools or selections.

Find a moderate to steep hill that's roughly 30-100 meters long. Think roughly 30-45 degree angle. This is the ideal, make do with what you have.

Wear a weight vest with 5-20lbs. I recommend starting with 0-5lbs for your very first session and adjusting from there.

Pick 1-3 exercises.

Jog up and down the hill continuously at a relaxed pace. Every time you hit the top, perform 10-20 reps of an exercise. Only one exercise is done at the top, rotate through your cluster.

Perform Peggy for 30-120 minutes

Sample Exercise Clusters:

    Push-Ups + Squats + Kettlebell Renegade Rows

    Kettlebell Swings + Push-Ups

    KB/DB Overhead Press + Leg Raises

    Burpees

    KB Snatch + KB Deadlift

> **Advanced Version:** Do one exercise at the top and another at the bottom. For example, kettlebell swings at the top and push-ups at the bottom. And/or use a heavier weight vest, heavier kettlebell etc.

Peggy is a great way to get in extra strength-endurance work. If there's a particular exercise you need more of in your life – include it. Choose movements that make sense for your goals. Consider selections that have you lifting logs overhead or holding rifles out in front of you. Peggy can help you apply specificity toward that kind of scenario. Get creative.

Peggy is not a hill sprint session. It's done continuously in low-gear, at a sustainable jog. Start with 30-45 minutes, work your way up to 90-120 as needed. Peggy isn't pretty. You'll probably spend a lot of time not being continuous. You might find yourself taking time outs, doubled over on jelly legs. All good, keep chipping away. When you can no longer jog, walk. The magic is still happening. Peggy can be used in place of any Hill or Ruck session. If rucking isn't a high priority, Peggy is the perfect substitute.

HILL SUBSTITUTES

Ultra runner Zach Miller trained for and won the JFK 50 Mile race while working on a cruise ship. He used the stairwells and treadmill while at sea. Where there's a will, there's a way.

If you don't have access to mountains and hills get creative. Stairs in buildings, stadiums, and the treadmill are all options. Longer stairways are an excellent substitute for Continuous Hill Runs.

A couple treadmill alternatives to get you thinking. Warmup and cooldown for each session. 10 minutes of flat jogging before and after is usually sufficient:

Continuous Hill Run/Indoor

Like the standard CHR but done on a treadmill. Only difference is you don't get the descent training.

Set elevation at 10-15% grade. 15% is usually the highest elevation setting.

Jog continuously at a relaxed sustainable pace for 30-120 minutes.

2/1 Indoor Hills

Use a high incline setting on the treadmill, somewhere between 10-15% grade.

Wear a 10lb-20lb weight vest (optional)

Jog 2 Minutes Easy Pace / Run 1 Minute Fast Pace

Perform for 30-120 Minutes

The easy pace should feel like a 4-5 out of 10, the fast pace roughly 7-8. Jog 'uphill' slowly for 2 minutes, then pick up the pace and intensity for 1. Repeat.

Vertical Tempo Run

Use a high incline setting on the treadmill, between 10-15% grade.

Run continuously at tempo pace for 20-40 minutes.

LONG RUN

The Long Run as the name suggests is the longest run of the week. Aside from the obvious cardiovascular benefits it has several other objectives:

Increases the boundaries of your longest run in an incremental fashion.

Conditions the body for off-road movement and work (like rucking).

Adds specificity. Most military dismounted locomotion is conducted off the beaten path, be it for operations or selection.

During Foundation LRs are prescribed in miles. During Continuation you can program them any way you like, distance or duration.

The LR is almost identical to LSS. It's run it at the same easy pace, but longer. Do the LR off-road/on a trail with elevation. Hilly terrain and occasional steep climbs are perfect but make do with what you have. Drop the heartrate parameters. Jog at an easy pace (RPE 4-5), exert a low level of effort. Jog the hills you can, power-hike any sections that are too steep. Rule of thumb: if you can see over the incline, jog it. If you can't, hike it.

THE MAGIC PILL: BACK TO BACK LONG RUNS

I stole this practice from the ultra running community. B2Bs are extremely potent when used wisely. As the name suggests, two Long Runs are done on consecutive days. B2Bs will turn your legs into steel, ramp up your conditioning, and boost your mental game in a massive way.

B2Bs have a way of shifting the paradigm in your head. Doing a couple 12-15 milers over the weekend makes a single 20 miler almost easy. Do back to back 20 milers, and a marathon or even ultra suddenly becomes very much within reach. The physical benefits and mental lessons are invaluable for schools and selections. You'll come to realize no matter how tired or sore you think you are you can still keep putting one leg in front of the other. Once you get warmed up things aren't as bad as they seem. After the recovery period, it'll feel like you received the benefits of a months worth of running compressed over two days. B2Bs are exceptional for your endurance game but MUST be used sparingly. Don't overdo them and don't rely on them at the expense of consistent shorter runs. Back to Back Long Runs are displayed in **BOLD.**

WEIGHT VEST RUN

If you're an operational athlete with little or no ruck requirement (like police special operations), the weight vest or plate carrier run is a good substitute. The ideal weight-vest run consists of slow trail jogging intermittently disrupted by uphill hiking.

Weighted running has several benefits for the operational athlete.

It increases bone density and strengthens the systems involved in load bearing.

It adds an element of specificity for operational athletes who wear body armor, duty belts, bunker gear, breaching tools etc.

It enhances unweighted running.

Find a trail with a few hills or gently rolling terrain. Hills are a natural way to buffer impact. They spread the wealth, so it's not the same muscles/joints/connective tissue being beaten repetitively like when running on flat ground. Not only is it good for injury prevention, but there's greater strength and muscular-endurance benefit. Avoid doing weighted runs on pavement.

Start with approximately 5-10lbs.

Weight-Vest running can potentially be hard on the body if you try and do too much at once or use too much weight. Exercise some common sense. Start light. Add more weight as you get a feel for how your body responds. Test the waters. Begin with 30 minutes and increase the duration as you become proficient. Stay on the trails/dirt to minimize impact. Break up your jog by walking the inclines.

RUCK

The objective of the long or conventional ruck is to complete the assigned distance/load. Speed is secondary but can be incorporated as needed. For example, if you're assigned an 8 mile ruck and you're comfortable with the distance/load, set a certain pace as the objective. You can also use portions of the ruck to test speed. For example, test a new pace during the middle 3 miles of that 8 mile ruck. Long rucks are primarily for building skill and increasing distance and load.

SPEED RUCK

Speed Ruck sessions are relatively short, ranging from 2-6 miles. Use them to work on your pace. Some benchmarks to aim for:

Basic/Beginner

Work toward a 15 minute/mile pace with 35lbs. When you own it, start working toward the intermediate benchmark.

Intermediate

Work toward a 13-14 minute/mile with 50-60lbs. When you achieve it, move on to the advanced benchmark.

Advanced

Work toward an 11-12 minute/mile with 50-70lbs.

How high you go depends on what you're training for. If you're preparing for conventional army or tactical law enforcement, you'll be fine hitting the basic or intermediate benchmarks. If you're aiming higher, start wrapping your ahead around the advanced standards.

DELOAD

Roughly every fourth or seventh week in Green Protocol is a deload or recovery week. Training is drastically reduced or stopped.

Deloads allow your body to heal from the previous cycle of training. Taking a step back prevents overuse injuries and burnout. It recharges body and mind for the next challenging block. You need to allow the training adaptations to happen so you can keep progressing beyond your normal limitations. Adaptation can't occur if you keep breaking yourself down. It occurs at rest during the recovery process.

There are several ways to approach deload weeks, none of them carved in stone:

For strength training, cut loads down to roughly 40%RM. Use minimal sets and keep the reps low (5 or less).

For SE, use 20-30% Max Reps and do half the prescribed circuits. Take the weight vest off.

Running is usually prescribed for deload weeks throughout Foundation, but when it isn't, cut volume and/or duration in half.

Another approach is to drop ALL training for the week and focus on mobility drills, stretching, and other rejuvenating activities. This is a good approach for experienced trainees that have taken a beating over the years.

Deload weeks are placed at recommended points in each template. They're not hard and fast rules. If you know what you're doing, skip the occasional deload, or do them every 6 weeks instead of every 3, etc. Be cautious, this is one instance where listening to your body isn't always smart. It's better to take a deload before you need one, not when you're falling apart. An injury isn't a sign to deload. Also don't fall into the insidious trap of feeling really good during a deload and turning a light workout into a PR setting session. Sometimes your energy skyrockets due to the drastically reduced work. You might get carried away and start trying to set new records. The problem is the increases in energy don't always accurately reflect the state of your body. You'll hit the gym for a light session, feel great, decide to keep adding plates to the bar – boom – that's when sprains, strains and tears occur.

APPLY A SENSE OF PLAY

I spent part of my childhood on a farm and did a lot of typical farm kid stuff – BB guns, minibikes, and chores galore. One pastime I picked up was archery. I bought a cheap bow, the kind that came with three arrows. I set a paper target up on a bale of hay and would spend hours shooting. Three arrows run out real fast, so I conned my little brother into running back and forth every few minutes to fetch them for me. Can't remember what I promised him or if I even delivered. He can thank me for his cardio though (the first TB client?). Here's the thing. Some days I would be out there for hours. Other days maybe just 10 minutes. Some days I wouldn't shoot at all. There was no structure, no formal drills, I adjusted and changed up my approach based on boredom and my evolving skillset. My accuracy got better and better, so I automatically started working on speed. When I got my speed *and* accuracy down, I started moving and shooting, switching hands, or trick shooting. Much of the time I'd just go back to straightforward stationary shooting. I spent the entire summer practicing. I got very, very good. I was practically Robin Hood, hitting arrow-on-arrow bullseyes. My arrows were too cheap to split anything but paper though, so they would just bounce off each other. Relatively speaking, no formal range day or rigid program matched what months of unstructured play did for my skills and sense of competence.

Of course, structure and programming is a necessary evil in the adult world. But you can borrow and apply that sense of play to aspects of training, particularly your endurance training: Long Runs, Peggy's Hills, rucks, Fartlek, etc. Treat them like playtime, not a workout you have to tick off at all costs. Don't approach them in an inflexible business-like manner.

Once upon a time I hit the trails for a hilly 25 km run. I was tired. I'd accumulated a bunch of volume the week leading up and was coming off nights. My legs were dead, and I didn't have much pep. Last thing I wanted to do was go for a run. I didn't go into it with a 'must crush' this attitude or try to psyche myself up. I decided I'd relax, have a little fun and ease into it. I gave myself permission to walk the entire thing or turn around at any point if I wanted to. I started out by walking the first kilometer, a gravel path that led to the trail proper. Normally I start running right away but screw it, not this time. After that first kilometer I finally started jogging, and I use the term jogging loosely. It was more like a zombie shuffle, not much faster than my walk. I did that for another couple kilometers. I started feeling better, my speed picked up automatically. But I was still a little dead-legged. Some of the inclines I normally ran, I stopped and walked. When I got to the highest point of elevation near the halfway mark, I stopped the clock, sat down for 5 minutes, ate some gel, and enjoyed the view. I pressed on. Toward the end I was feeling rejuvenated and could have easily surpassed the 25k mark. It turned into one of the best runs of the month. It was a near-perfect endurance building session by any measure. My heartrate stayed centered in the 'correct' zone because of the intermittent walking and stopping. I got specific-strength and muscular-endurance training by way of moving over the hills. Whether I was hiking or jogging the ascents, it didn't matter, I got the benefits either way. Was it technically a '25km *run*'? No, it was maybe

22kms of running, with the remainder being hiking or walking. But it was a full 25km of *endurance training*.

Don't look at your endurance runs like rigid little torture sessions that have to be robotically completed in an overly structured manner. Cultivate a sense of curiosity around your performance, like a child fooling around with a new soccer ball in the driveway, or a dude taking his surfboard out into the ocean. Think of your training as endurance-play rather than endurance work. Some of your runs will be more purposeful, others will be more playful. Some might start out playful and end up purposeful. The type of endurance we want is built over time by accumulating higher and higher volume in a sustainable fashion. Get used to using different mental gears for different domains.

FOUNDATION

"Step by step, walk the thousand mile road."

Musashi, Book of Five Rings

CAPACITY

"That's been one of my mantras – focus and simplicity. Simple can be harder than complex; you have to work hard to get your thinking clean to make it simple."

Steve Jobs

OBJECTIVES

Strength/Hypertrophy

Base Aerobic Fitness

Benchmark: 6 Mile Run/60 Minutes

OVERVIEW

Capacity is the cornerstone of Foundation. This is where we start building raw strength and aerobic fitness. The more general fitness you have, the more you can channel into combat fitness.

Capacity is nothing but lifting and easy steady-state running. If you're into simple approaches with big results, you'll love it. If you're a variety junkie, you probably won't.

Capacity has a relatively easy benchmark: a 6 mile run in 60 minutes or less. Guidelines are provided for extending Capacity if the benchmark isn't met.

There are three versions, the standard approach, and two modified templates for special cases.

The standard template is a 50/50 split between lifting and running.

The hypertrophy variant starts with a mass building block before transitioning to standard programming. This one's for the underweight hardgainer. Or the classic 'slow twitch' athlete that has a handle on running but struggles with building muscle and strength.

The increased running version is the opposite. If you're convinced squats give you all the cardio you need, this is for you. If you get winded going up the stairs this is for you. If you don't take the stairs – for you. It's also a good choice if you're preparing for a particularly challenging endurance based school, and running is your kryptonite.

Capacity can be used as an alternative to *Tactical Barbell's* Base Building template.

Capacity can be cut down to 8 weeks for trainees that have already spent a significant amount of time on this kind of base training and can meet the benchmark.

CAPACITY

Week	Day 1	Day 2	Day 3	Day 4	Day 5	Day 6	Day 7
				CAPACITY			
1	OP	30-60	OP	30-60	OP	60-90	
2	OP	30-60	OP	30-60	OP	60-90	
3	OP	30-60	OP	30-60	OP	60-90	
4	Deload	30		30		30	
5	OP	60-90	OP	60-90	OP	90-120	
6	OP	60-90	OP	60-90	OP	90-120	
7	OP	60-90	OP	60-90	OP	90-120	
8	Deload	30		30		30	
9	OP	60-120	OP	60-120	OP	120+	
10	OP	60-120	OP	60-120	OP	120+	
11	OP	60-120	OP	60-120	OP	120+	
12		30		30		6 Mile	

NOTES

Capacity consists of strength training and LSS running.

OP: Op/PRO, Op/DUP, or standard Operator can be used.

LSS Running is prescribed in minutes. 30-60 = LSS run for 30 to 60 minutes.

Consider using the easy/hard principle when determining LSS duration. Alternate between longer and shorter sessions. Listen to your body.

Additional LSS Runs can be performed on OP days before or after the session or AM/PM. 20-30 minutes or more.

During Capacity get a bit stricter with the LSS runs. Stay in the lower end of the aerobic range and jog on flat terrain.

LSS doubles as active recovery.

Capacity can be cut down to 8 weeks for trainees that have already spent a significant amount of time on this kind of base training and can meet the benchmark. Use the first or last 8 weeks, depending on how much running you want.

BENCHMARK

Perform a 6 Mile Run in 60 minutes or less. The run can be performed on road or flat surface.

Congrats – you are now eligible to move on to Velocity. If you can't meet the benchmark, see the "Remedial" section.

MODIFICATIONS

This section contains modified versions of Capacity for people that need more loving attention in one area or another.

If running comes relatively easy but you struggle with building strength and muscle, use the increased hypertrophy version of Capacity.

If you're a gym rat or 'fast twitch' athlete and have your sights set on something endurance-heavy like the combat arms, use the increased running variant.

If you're somewhere in the middle go with the standard template. If you're not sure where you stand go with the standard template. If you're not particularly strong OR good at running - standard template. This is just one step in a lengthy process, don't overthink it.

Know your objective. Is it endurance-heavy like Ranger school? Or is it more middle of the road like police special operations? If your objective lies on the extreme end of the spectrum, using a specialized variant might be the way to go. Next, assess your weaknesses in relation to the objective. If you struggle with cardio *and* your goal is endurance-heavy, go with the increased running template. If you're underweight and crumble under a heavy ruck or bunker gear, the increased hypertrophy variant might be of interest. When in doubt, stick with the standard template.

| \multicolumn{8}{c}{CAPACITY/Hypertrophy} |
Week	Day 1	Day 2	Day 3	Day 4	Day 5	Day 6	Day 7
1	Zulu	Zulu		Zulu	Zulu		
2	Zulu	Zulu		Zulu	Zulu		
3	Zulu	Zulu		Zulu	Zulu		
4	Deload						
5	OP	30-60	OP	30-60	OP	60-90	
6	OP	30-60	OP	30-60	OP	60-90	
7	OP	30-60	OP	30-60	OP	60-90	
8	Deload	30		30		30	
9	OP	60-90	OP	60-90	OP	90-120	
10	OP	60-90	OP	60-90	OP	90-120	
11	OP	60-90	OP	60-90	OP	90-120	
12	Deload	30		30		6 Mile	

NOTES

Zulu: Zulu/HT. Tactical Barbell MASS Protocol, or any mass building program can be used.

Keep conditioning minimal during Zulu block. No more than 2-3 conditioning sessions per week. Brief HIIT/HIC/Metcon style sessions or easy LSS for 30-45 minutes. Put any surplus time and energy into Zulu: extra sets, accessory work etc.

CAPACITY / More Running								
Week	Day 1	Day 2	Day 3	Day 4	Day 5	Day 6	Day 7
1	FT	30-60	30-60	FT	30-60	60-90	
2	FT	30-60	30-60	FT	30-60	60-90	
3	FT	30-60	30-60	FT	30-60	60-90	
4	Deload	30		30		30	
5	FT	60-90	60-90	FT	60-90	90-120	
6	FT	60-90	60-90	FT	60-90	90-120	
7	FT	60-90	60-90	FT	60-90	90-120	
8	Deload	30		30		30	
9	FT	60-120	60-120	FT	60-120	120+	
10	FT	60-120	60-120	FT	60-120	120+	
11	FT	60-120	60-120	FT	60-120	120+	
12		30		30		6 Mile	

NOTES

FT: Fighter Template is used for the strength component in this variant.

Extra LSS can be done on Fighter days, before/after lifting or AM/PM style.

ABBREVIATED

Capacity can be whittled down into an 8 week template. This version is generally used as an alternative to Base Building or when coupled with Continuation templates like C/CAT. You can also abbreviate it if you've just come off a standard Tactical Barbell Base Building block and don't want to spend a ton of extra time on similar domains. Any variant can be abbreviated. If you're a beginner, I recommend the full version for your first go-around.

Week	Day 1	Day 2	Day 3	Day 4	Day 5	Day 6	Day 7
			CAPACITY				
1	OP	30-60	OP	30-60	OP	60-90	
2	OP	30-60	OP	30-60	OP	60-90	
3	OP	30-60	OP	30-60	OP	60-90	
4	Deload	30		30		30	
5	OP	60-90	OP	60-90	OP	90-120	
6	OP	60-90	OP	60-90	OP	90-120	
7	OP	60-90	OP	60-90	OP	90-120	
8	Deload	30		30		6 Mile	

In this example I used the first 8 weeks, but you can also use the last 8 to squeeze more running out of it.

When using Capacity for Base Building or Continuation, the benchmark test can be dropped.

REMEDIAL

If you can't meet the benchmark, do this. Switch to the increased running version. Incorporate speedwork as shown below. Repeat the three week remedial block until the benchmark is met:

\multicolumn{8}{c	}{Capacity/Remedial}
9	FT	MR 2-3	90-120	FT	90-120	120+	
10	FT	MR 3-4	90-120	FT	90-120	120+	
11	FT	MR 4-5	90-120	FT	90-120	120+	
12		30		30			6 Mile

Focus on quality reps with the speedwork.

VELOCITY

'If you want to be a successful runner, you have to consider everything. It's no good just thinking about endurance and not to develop fine speed. Likewise – it's no good training for speed, or anaerobic capacity with lots of interval type training when you haven't developed your aerobic capacity to maximum. You have to take a long view and train on all aspects of development through a systematic program. It's a lot of hard work for five, six, or seven years. There's no secret formula. There's no shortcut to the top.'

Arthur Lydiard

ULTRARUNNING: LESSONS LEARNED

Prior to writing this book I ran my first ultra. It's the closest I've come in the civilian world to feeling like I was on a selection. It was all about managing mental and physical resources moment to moment. As a middle aged has-been my results were nothing to brag about, but I learned valuable new lessons and was reminded of important old ones. Green Protocol is not an ultrarunning program, but principles and techniques from that community are incorporated because it's an almost perfect fit for military fitness. Ultra runners train for endurance, terrain, and speed, in suitable ratios for combat arms work.

Reminders and lessons (re)learned:

Consistent, frequent running is key. Running shorter distances regularly is better than relying on the weekly Long Run and being inconsistent with the others.

Elevation is a game changer. Being comfortable, fast, and competent on a flat run is not the same as being faced with irregular terrain or vert. Elevation can cut your pace in half and double the speed at which fatigue sets in. Unlike typical running events, ultras often include significant climbs. Ultra runners specifically train ascents and descents. Likewise, military work is usually done offroad on challenging terrain. Harsh schools and selections often make use of mountains to weed out candidates. Running and moving over hills is one of the best ways to improve combat fitness. As we discussed in an earlier chapter, running lays the foundation for rucking – and offroad/uphill running is that much more applicable than flat road or trail.

Elevation builds legs of steel. No big surprise, running up and down hills has a hypertrophic effect. Many of the ultra runners I saw had massive quads and calves relative to their road marathon counterparts. My own leg strength, muscular-endurance, and body composition improved significantly after incorporating targeted hill work. These are specific adaptations that simply can't be replicated by squats and isolated SE training.

Elevation is your friend. The cardiovascular and specific strength benefits are unparalleled for combat fitness. Seek it out and incorporate it in your training. Green Protocol includes a substantial amount of vertical training along with guidelines for sprinkling it in your regular runs/rucks.

Downhill training is almost as important as uphill work. Running or hiking downhill for lengthy periods of time can quickly take your legs out of the game if you're not prepared. Your muscles, joints and connective tissue are being hit from angles you probably don't experience very often. Being able to move downhill quickly is a massive benefit if you're performing a timed ruck or run – it helps make up for time lost on the uphills. The good news is it doesn't take much descent training to have an impact. Green Protocol incorporates downhill training through specific hill sessions and regular runs/rucks.

Back-to-Back Long Runs are a cheat code. When used wisely. This is one of the most valuable tools I picked up from the ultra community. The back to back is a force multiplier for running and general endurance. Back-to-Backs teach you your body is capable of much more than your mind wants you to believe. You might be hobbling around and completely depleted on the day of the second run, but once you get going, you'll see that you can keep putting one leg in front of the other. See any applicability to selection? This isn't just about the mental stuff. Your endurance and running ability will skyrocket after the recovery period. After back-to-back 20-30ks, a single 40k or 50k becomes significantly easier. Back to Back runs and rucks are prescribed throughout Green Protocol. You'll love what they do for you.

Strength training is important but must be used strategically. I was reminded of how valuable a minimalist template like Fighter is within an endurance context. It significantly boosted my performance on the ascents/descents and built overall resilience. At times my weekly mileage was three times higher than normal, yet I remained injury free. I could do a heavy squat session the day before a hilly 30km run with little issue due to Fighter's submaximal/minimal approach. In contrast, one of my running partners, 15 years my junior, was doing the 'wrong' kind of lifting. He was in the gym four times a week using a program with regular maximum effort lifts and a high amount of volume and assistance work. He was overly attached to his muscle and feared it would all disappear if he didn't annihilate himself in the gym. He didn't know how to pivot and change his priorities based on the objective. He was placing equal importance on weight training at a time when running should have taken priority. He was constantly sidelined with minor overuse injuries or fatigue and missed too many training runs. On race day, he was unable to finish. Didn't even make it halfway. Didn't meet the first checkpoint timing and was pulled off the course.

Know when to pull back on the strength training. Stop the heavy lifting when the weekly mileage starts peaking. Switching to bodyweight or weighted calisthenics is usually a good strategy when run volume is at it's highest. Bear in mind this is within the context of heavy endurance training. It doesn't necessarily apply to a 10k or even half-marathon. Initially when you stop weight training, you'll notice how much easier it is to run. But, if you stop for too long, you'll also notice the benefits go away: durability, speed, and ease of movement over elevation. It's a question of balancing the pros and cons by way of timing. We want the benefits of weight training with minimal impact on running. These principles are incorporated throughout Green Protocol.

A proper taper is gold Jerry- Gold! Trying to do significant training within two weeks of an event won't help and can potentially hurt your game. It's too late for any meaningful new adaptation to set in. You're just prolonging the state of breakdown the body's in and setting yourself up for injury. Instead, let your body heal and adapt from all the training it's done up to that point. Your performance will skyrocket. In my younger days, I've been guilty of trying to squeeze in a few panicky sessions a couple days or even the night before an important PFT or event. Contrast that with times I didn't, and it's night and day. In this instance I tapered properly before the ultra. My legs felt unbreakable on the day. I had more energy than I was used to. I flew over the first half of the course which included significant elevation and kept waiting for the pain and fatigue in my legs to set in. The pain eventually arrived of course, but at a much later point than it normally did on training runs.

This Too Shall Pass aka 'Downhill Victory Speeches & Uphill Excuses'. It was comical watching how predictably my mind played games with me. The race I participated in had a decent amount of elevation gain, around 2500 meters. The only flat portions were a few kms on the front and back end. On top of that this was deemed the hardest version of the race ever put on due to 150mm of rainfall. Covid had bumped this race up farther in the year than normal. Despite that, during the downhills and flats I felt great. It was easy, I was moving quickly, and my fatigue disappeared. Positive emotions and mental chatter emerged. I was preparing my victory speech; how much I appreciated my training partners, and how it wasn't as difficult as I anticipated. I would bathe in the admiration of my colleagues when I returned to the team. I would give them helpful tips for their own training. This ultra thing was overrated or maybe I really was special.

Then the uphills.

I would slow down drastically, my heart would pound, my legs didn't work. I was running on trails that had turned into streams. There was no way I was moving fast enough to meet upcoming cut-off times. The Hero Of Positivity vanished. A new voice emerged along with that sinking feeling of looming potential failure. I started preparing my excuses. This is my first ultra. I've always been a fast-twitch athlete anyway, I may suck at this - but no one can beat me at a hundred meter sprint. Maybe I should fake an injury. I wasn't able to prepare enough because I have a tough job and work nightshifts. Everyone else here has the time to train, they don't have to deal with what I deal with. I'll give up now and take the loss, it's okay I'll train even harder for it next time. I've already accomplished lots of other equally difficult things in my life, it isn't a big deal if fail at this one little thing, I've earned it.

Thankfully this wasn't my first rodeo. I recognized both voices as imposters and let them yak away in the background. I knew if I just held on whatever I was feeling would pass. Don't get too excited when things feel easy, don't fall into a pit of depression when things get tough. One foot in front of the other, this too shall pass. You'll run into this kind of mental chatter frequently when preparing for or performing in the roles this book is aimed at. If you have selections/schools under your belt, you're likely already very familiar with this. Proper training and preparation will delay the arrival of these two clowns but make no mistake they will eventually visit. Be aware and learn to deal with them accordingly.

VELOCITY

OBJECTIVES

Running

Maximal-Strength

Strength-Endurance

Benchmark: 20 Mile Run / Challenge: 27 Mile Run

OVERVIEW

Velocity consists of four runs per week across several key categories: speedwork, elevation training, and long easy mileage. LSS runs build weekly mileage and facilitate recovery. Speedwork is geared for longer distances. Hill training conditions you for offroad movement and builds specific strength. Weekly Long Runs extend the limit of your overall endurance. Back-to-Back Long Runs are prescribed at various points to significantly increase base endurance and work capacity.

Fighter Template is used for the strength training component of Velocity. Lifting is performed twice a week, which allows for a greater focus on running. Toward the end of the phase, when mileage is at it's peak, the heavy lifting is replaced with strength-endurance training. SE training takes less of a toll on the body and nervous system, making the high mileage running more manageable. In addition to improving muscular endurance, SE training has a positive impact on cardiovascular fitness, amplifying the effect of the programming. All the systems in your body will be pulling in the same direction for once.

There is a gradual progression across domains/sessions. Mileage, repetitions, rounds, and load are increased incrementally over the block. Every fourth week is Deload. Training breaks your body down. Deload weeks give your body a chance to repair and build back stronger to face the next level of challenge.

Velocity can be modified in several ways. It can be abbreviated for those that don't need 20 mile capability. It can be abbreviated for experienced runners that don't need to start with low mileage. It can be run in Easy Mode. It can be modified for more or less Strength-Endurance training.

At the end of the block, you'll be required to complete a 20 mile offroad run in 8 hours or less. Alternatively, you can do the 27 mile challenge.

VELOCITY

Week	Day 1	Day 2	Day 3	Day 4	Day 5	Day 6	Day 7
1	FT	LSS 5	TPO 3-5	FT	LSS 3	LR 8	
2	FT	LSS 6	Hill	FT	LSS 3	LR 9	
3	FT	LSS 6	800/3-5	FT	LSS 3	LR 10	
4	Deload	LSS 3		LSS 3		LSS 3	
5	FT	LSS 6	TPO 3-5	FT	LSS 4	LR 11	
6	FT	LSS 8	Hill	FT	LSS 4	LR 12	
7	FT	LSS 8	800/3-5	FT		**LR 13**	**LR 8**
8	Deload	LSS 4		LSS 4		LSS 4	
9	FT	LSS 7	TPO 3-5	FT	LSS 5	LR 14	
10	FT	LSS 10	Hill	FT	LSS 5	LR 15	
11	FT	LSS 10	800/5-8	FT		**LR 16**	**LR 10**
12	Deload	LSS 5		LSS 5		LSS 5	
13	SE	LSS 8	TPO 3-5	SE	LSS 6	LR 17	
14	SE	LSS 12	Hill	SE	LSS 6	LR 18	
15	SE	LSS 12	800/5-8	SE		**LR 19**	**LR 12**
16	Taper	LSS 2		LSS 2		LSS 3	
17		LSS 3		LSS 2		LSS 2	**LR 20**

NOTES

FT: Fighter Template

LSS: Prescribed in Miles. Easy trail run.

TPO: Tempo Run. Prescribed in Miles. Add 1 mile warmup/1 mile cooldown. Fartlek can be used in lieu of Tempo.

Hill: Perform 30-120 minutes of elevation training using any Hill session or Peggy

800: 800 Meter Repeats/# of rounds. Mile Repeats can also be used.

LR: Long Run. Performed offroad/with elevation. Fartlek can occasionally be used instead.

LR/LR: Back to Back Long Runs

SE: Strength Endurance Training/2 Day Template

Experienced runners can start later in the template. For example, begin the template at Week 5 instead of week 1.

Deload: the prescribed sessions are recommendations. Do less if needed. Walking, swimming, cycling etc. can be used instead of running.

BENCHMARK TESTING

Perform a 20 mile offroad run in 8 hours or less.

Hilly terrain/off-road trail is the standard but make do with what you have. Don't blow yourself out but cultivate a sense of curiosity around how fast you can finish under the allotted time. Doing an off-road 20 miler is a major milestone in and of itself regardless of time.

If you pass – congratulations. You're ready for the next phase. Take a week off and relax. Eat some junk, sleep in if possible. Waste a little time doing nothing productive. Don't step foot in a gym. This will give your body some rest, and more importantly your mind gets a break.

If you can't meet the benchmark, take a week off as above and restart Velocity at around week 9 or earlier.

CHALLENGE

Instead of 20 miles, test for 27. Perform the run offroad in 11 hours or less. Watch for the wall at around 20-25 miles. Keep moving, even if you have to speed walk or zombie shuffle. If you pass, congrats. You've technically run an ultramarathon distance, but don't go bragging about it just yet, actual ultras usually start at 50k/30 miles. If you've been consistent throughout Velocity, there is no doubt in my mind you will succeed.

FUELING

Fueling strategies can have a significant impact on your long runs and benchmark performance. Read the Fueling section at the end of this chapter.

MODIFICATIONS

Velocity can be modified in several ways.

It can be abbreviated.

It can be run in easy mode.

It can be modified for more or less Strength-Endurance (SE).

ABBREVIATED

Velocity can be whittled down into a shorter template with lower benchmarks. Not all operational roles require the endurance base a 20 mile run capability provides. 10 or 12 might be more than enough for your objective. If you don't need it don't waste time training for it. Spend that extra time training something relevant or use it to shore up weaknesses. Velocity is set-up so you can easily snip it at the benchmark you want.

\multicolumn{8}{c}{**VELOCITY**}
Week	Day 1	Day 2	Day 3	Day 4	Day 5	Day 6	Day 7
1	FT	LSS 5	TPO 3-5	FT	LSS 3	LR 8	
2	FT	LSS 6	Hill	FT	LSS 3	LR 9	
3	FT	LSS 6	800/3-5	FT	LSS 3	LR 10	
4	Deload	LSS 3		LSS 3		LSS 3	
5	FT	LSS 6	TPO 3-5	FT	LSS 4	LR 11	
6	FT	LSS 8	Hill	FT	LSS 4	LR 12	
7	FT	LSS 8	800/3-5	FT		**LR 13**	**LR 8**
8	Taper	LSS 2		LSS 2		LSS 3	
9		LSS 3		LSS 2		LSS 2	LR 15

All I did was cut it down the middle. It went from a 16 week protocol with a 20 mile benchmark to roughly half that time and 15 miles. Keep in mind you'll likely be able to run farther than the benchmark in both cases. It's the training you do over the weeks and months that's important, not any single benchmark run. Benchmarks are used as objective standards to ensure everyone gets a measurable baseline of success with this system.

SE can be subbed in for Fighter during weeks 5-7.

Velocity can also be abbreviated for experienced trainees. If you're coming in with a stronger running background start the template at a point that aligns with your abilities. In this example I lopped off the first four weeks. Our experienced runner starts at Week 5:

			VELOCITY				
Week	Day 1	Day 2	Day 3	Day 4	Day 5	Day 6	Day 7
5	FT	LSS 6	TPO 3-5	FT	LSS 4	LR 11	
6	FT	LSS 8	Hill	FT	LSS 4	LR 12	
7	FT	LSS 8	800/3-5	FT		**LR 13**	**LR 8**
8	Deload	LSS 4		LSS 4		LSS 4	
9	FT	LSS 7	TPO 3-5	FT	LSS 5	LR 14	
10	FT	LSS 10	Hill	FT	LSS 5	LR 15	
11	FT	LSS 10	800/5-8	FT		**LR 16**	**LR 10**
12	Deload	LSS 5		LSS 5		LSS 5	
13	SE	LSS 8	TPO 3-5	SE	LSS 6	LR 17	
14	SE	LSS 12	Hill	SE	LSS 6	LR 18	
15	SE	LSS 12	800/5-8	SE		**LR 19**	**LR 12**
16	Taper	LSS 2		LSS 2		LSS 3	

He starts the template at a point more relevant to his abilities, sharpens his skillset, and is ready to move on to Outcome.

EASY MODE

Put Velocity in ' Easy Mode' by cutting all of the distances/times in half:

\multicolumn{8}{c}{VELOCITY}
Week	Day 1	Day 2	Day 3	Day 4	Day 5	Day 6	Day 7
1	FT	LSS 2	TPO 2-3	FT	LSS 2	LR 4	
2	FT	LSS 3	Hill	FT	LSS 2	LR 4	
3	FT	LSS 3	800/2-4	FT	LSS 2	LR 5	
4	Deload	LSS 2		LSS 2		LSS 2	
5	FT	LSS 3	TPO 2-3	FT	LSS 2	LR 5	
6	FT	LSS 4	Hill	FT	LSS 2	LR 6	
7	FT	LSS 4	800/2-4	FT		**LR 7**	**LR 4**
8	Deload	LSS 2		LSS 2		LSS 2	
9	FT	LSS 4	TPO 2-3	FT	LSS 3	LR 7	
10	FT	LSS 5	Hill	FT	LSS 3	LR 8	
11	FT	LSS 5	800/4-6	FT		**LR 9**	**LR 5**
12	Deload	LSS 3		LSS 3		LSS 3	
13	SE	LSS 4	TPO 2-3	SE	LSS 4	LR 9	
14	SE	LSS 6	Hill	SE	LSS 4	LR 10	
15	SE	LSS 6	800/4-6	SE		**LR 11**	**LR 6**
16	Taper	LSS 2		LSS 2		LSS 3	
17		LSS 3		LSS 2		LSS 2	**LR 12**

I've rounded up or down to avoid half miles etc. Hill training can be done for 15-60 minutes.

HARD MODE?

If you're coming into Velocity with a serious ultra background or similar, you can roughly double the numbers and adjust the mileage spread as you see fit. If you're used to regular 50-70+ mile weeks, you're experienced enough to program your own running. Layer in Fighter template and SE, adjust the hill training and speedwork, and you're good to go.

MORE STRENGTH-ENDURANCE

Velocity can be tailored for more or less strength-endurance. Strength-Endurance is a strength domain therefore it changes places with other strength domains. If you want more of it, sub it in for Fighter template in three week blocks:

\	\	\	VELOCITY	\	\	\	\
Week	Day 1	Day 2	Day 3	Day 4	Day 5	Day 6	Day 7
1	FT	LSS 5	TPO 3-5	FT	LSS 3	LR 8	
2	FT	LSS 6	Hill	FT	LSS 3	LR 9	
3	FT	LSS 6	800/3-5	FT	LSS 3	LR 10	
4	Deload	LSS 3		LSS 3		LSS 3	
5	FT	LSS 6	TPO 3-5	FT	LSS 4	LR 11	
6	FT	LSS 8	Hill	FT	LSS 4	LR 12	
7	FT	LSS 8	800/3-5	FT		**LR 13**	**LR 8**
8	Deload	LSS 4		LSS 4		LSS 4	
9	**SE**	LSS 7	TPO 3-5	**SE**	LSS 5	LR 14	
10	**SE**	LSS 10	Hill	**SE**	LSS 5	LR 15	

11	**SE**	LSS 10	800/5-8	**SE**		**LR 16**	**LR 10**
12	Deload	LSS 5		LSS 5		LSS 5	
13	SE	LSS 8	TPO 3-5	SE	LSS 6	LR 17	
14	SE	LSS 12	Hill	SE	LSS 6	LR 18	
15	SE	LSS 12	800/5-8	SE		**LR 19**	**LR 12**
16	Taper	LSS 2		LSS 2		LSS 3	
17		LSS 3		LSS 2		**LR 20**	

In this example our hypothetical trainee is preparing for a tactical law enforcement unit that has no ruck component. Running, work capacity, strength, and muscular-endurance, are going to be priorities for this particular selection. Based on his self-assessment and timeline, he's decided to skip Outcome. He'll use Capacity and follow it up with this Velocity variant. He'll use Peggy for most of his Hill sessions. SE is a personal weak point, so he swaps in an extra block in lieu of Fighter. That gives him a solid six weeks of SE prior to selection. More than enough for his objective.

NO STRENGTH ENDURANCE

For no SE at all, replace it with Fighter template. You'll be getting a substantial amount of SE during Outcome. Leaving it until then might make sense for your goals. If you like to keep things simple or want to maintain your progress with Fighter, leave it out.

FUELING

Proper fueling can extend performance, prevent dehydration, and stave off hyponatremia. Hyponatremia is when your sodium levels get too low, which can lead to the funky chicken or even death. Hyponatremia is generally caused by drinking too much water without electrolytes in hot weather during long or intense runs. Overdrinking flushes the sodium out of your system, and you end up getting jiggy with it.

Generally, this isn't a concern if you're running for 1 to 2 hours or less. In such cases water by itself (or nothing) is fine. Take the climate into account. If you're running in extreme heat, then even a 20-30 minute run might benefit from electrolytes. Long Runs are great for testing fueling strategies.

These are loose guidelines for runs or conditioning sessions that exceed 1-2 hours:

Every Hour/On the Hour:

50-60gms Fast Acting Carb

500mg Sodium + accompanying electrolytes

Sip Water or Gatorade throughout the rest of the run as needed.

Gels like GU or Hammer are convenient quick acting carbs. This is one of those times where sugar=good and can make the difference between finishing or not finishing a challenging run.

For sodium, something simple like Salt-Stick or NUUN tablets will do the job. They contain other required electrolytes like potassium in balanced ratios. 500mg is a loose guideline. Use more or less as needed.

Use a running vest/bladders filled with Gatorade or water. Count the number of gels you're going to use based on a rough estimate of how long you'll be out on the trail. Salt tabs or electrolytes can be stored in a small plastic pillbox. Pad the pillbox with cotton balls to avoid moisture and eliminate any rattling. Store your fuel in your vests/pockets.

Every hour on the hour eat one or two gel packs along with a salt tablet. Even if you don't feel like it, *especially* when you don't feel like it. Sip water/Gatorade throughout as needed.

Individual needs vary. You might need more or less carb, more or less electrolyte, etc. You might even prefer or have the ability to handle whole foods.

CAUTION

Some food for thought, bad pun sort of intended.

Certain schools include food/water/supplement restrictions, like SAPS Special Task Force or US Army Ranger school. STF candidates aren't allowed to eat for 90 hours during a hell week type portion of training. Ranger candidates are allowed only two MREs a day for around two months. Other schools and selections may have similar restrictions.

You might not have access to Gucci gels, supplements, potions, and pills. Don't get too attached to them in training. If gels and such start becoming a crutch or requirement, re-evaluate your approach and gradually expose yourself to training without. Don't do anything unsafe or stupid. It's one thing to limit gels or supplements, but don't go do a five hour run in the desert without water to 'test yourself'.

Being attached to a particular diet or food source is the same thing. The tougher schools/selections won't cater to your carnivore or vegan diet. Metabolic flexibility is key for the operational athlete.

OUTCOME

We should remember that one man is much the same as another, and that he is best who is trained in the severest school.

Thucydides

OBEJCTIVES

Ruck Proficiency

Strength/Muscular-Endurance

Work Capacity

Peaking Phase

Benchmark: 20 Mile Ruck + 50lbs / Challenge: Consecutive 20 Mile Ruck+ 10 Mile Run

OVERVIEW

Outcome is a two part 16 week template. The first 8 weeks consists of basic ruck training and work capacity building. Strength training is performed twice a week using Fighter template. Running is put on the back-burner to allow for a greater focus on rucking. Part 1 culminates with back to back 10 and 6 mile rucks with 35lbs.

Part 2 is Peak phase. It builds on part 1 but can also be detached and used standalone as a peaking block prior to schools/selection. Volume ramps up in the form of two-a-days and increasingly longer ruck sessions. Fighter template is replaced with strength-endurance training to add specificity. Speedwork is performed regularly to ensure you're prepared for timed events. The final benchmark is a 20 mile ruck with 50lbs. Prior to benchmark testing you'll be doing regular back-to-back ruck sessions. Peak includes a built-in taper leading up to the benchmark test. It can also be used to lead up to your school or event.

Outcome is a versatile template. For many, doing the first 8 weeks will be enough. For more challenging goals doing the full template is the way to go. Whether you do the full thing or just half, you can use Peak anytime as a self-contained pre-event template. For example, your event is still many months away and doesn't mesh with the end of Outcome. Do Part 1, then transition to a Continuation template to maintain a holding pattern. Switch to Peak when you get close enough to your event. Likewise, you can do Outcome fully (including Peak), switch to Continuation, and repeat Peak prior to your event. I don't want to get ahead of myself here, but you can also use just the first half of Peak. It becomes a shorter sharpening phase, but still provides a substantial amount of strength-endurance training, work capacity, and rucking. It might be the right fit if the full thing is overkill for your particular goal. It can also act as a brief touch-up if you've maintained an appropriate level of readiness. More on this in the Modifications section.

NO RUCK/MINIMAL RUCK

Don't need to ruck much? Don't need to ruck at all? Rucking aside, Outcome brings value by building significant work capacity and muscular endurance through the two-a-days, SE training, and other sessions like Peggy's Hills. That said, if you're preparing for a selection/school with minimal/no ruck component, you can substitute more relevant sessions for some or all of the rucks. Swimming, weight vest runs, Long Runs, hill work, and other forms of training can be subbed in. All of this will be covered in Modifications.

OUTCOME

				OUTCOME			
Week	Day 1	Day 2	Day 3	Day 4	Day 5	Day 6	Day 7
1	FT	S/Ruck 2	LSS	FT	FK 5	Ruck 4	
2	FT	S/Ruck 2	LSS	FT	Peggy	Ruck 5	
3	FT	S/Ruck 2	LSS	FT		**Ruck 6**	**Ruck 4**
4	Deload	LSS		LSS		LSS	
5	FT	S/Ruck 4	LSS	FT	FK 5	Ruck 8	
6	FT	S/Ruck 4	LSS	FT	Peggy	Ruck 9	
7	FT	S/Ruck 4	LSS	FT		**Ruck 10**	**Ruck 6**
8	Deload	LSS		LSS		LSS	
				PEAK			
9	SE (LSS)	S/Ruck 6	SE (LSS)	MR 3-5	SE (LSS)	Ruck 12	
10	SE (LSS)	S/Ruck 6	SE (LSS)	Hill	SE (LSS)	Ruck 13	
11	SE (LSS)	S/Ruck 6	SE (LSS)		SE	**Ruck 14**	**Ruck 8**
12	Deload	LSS		LSS		LSS	
13	SE (LSS)	S/Ruck 8	SE (LSS)	MR 3-5	SE (LSS)	Ruck 16	
14	SE (LSS)	S/Ruck 8	SE (LSS)	Hill	SE (LSS)	Ruck 17	
15	SE (LSS)	S/Ruck 8	SE (LSS)		SE	**Ruck 18**	**Ruck 10**
16	Taper	LSS		LSS		LSS	
17		LSS		LSS		**Ruck 20**	

NOTES

FT: Fighter Template

SE: Strength-Endurance Training/3 Day Template

S/Ruck: Speed Ruck (Miles)

Ruck: Miles

LSS: 60-120 Minute Run. Listen to your body. Do lower or higher end of the range accordingly.

LSS/Deload Weeks: 30-45 Minutes. Other modes of LSS can be used here, cycling, swimming, easy hiking, walking, etc.

LSS/Taper Weeks: 30 Minutes

FK: Fartlek (Miles)

MR: Mile Repeats 3 to 5 reps.

Peggy: 30-120 minutes.

Hill: 30-120 minutes using any hill session: CHR, Peggy, Vert Ladders, etc.

SE (LSS): Two-A-Days. Strength Endurance Training + LSS Run. Sessions can be performed together, or at different times of the day such as an AM/PM set-up. 30-90 minutes of LSS is recommended during two-a-days.

During **PEAK** phase speedwork (Mile Repeats, 400M, etc.) can replace Hill sessions if needed.

RUCK/LOAD PROGRESSION

Rucking is hard on the body. Start LIGHT and build up slowly!

Week 1-3: 30lbs

Week 5-7: 35lbs

Week 9-11: 40lbs

Week 13-15: 45lbs

Week 17 (Benchmark): 50lbs

Can be adjusted for experience. Experienced trainees can start with heavier increments or the full 50lbs. If you're struggling, start lower, around 15-20lbs.

BENCHMARK TESTING

Perform a 20 mile ruck with 50lbs at or near the target pace you've been working toward. Do it on hilly terrain if possible.

CHALLENGE

Perform 20 mile ruck/50lbs at or near target pace. Drop the ruck at the finish line and immediately perform a 10 mile run for time.

MODIFICATIONS

Not everyone is going to need a 20 mile ruck benchmark or high volume two-a-day training. Outcome can be modified/customized to align with your goals:

It can be abbreviated.

It can be customized to incorporate specific skillsets like swimming.

It can be customized to minimize or eliminate rucking (tactical law enforcement, specialty Fire, etc.)

ABBREVIATED

OUTCOME/8 Weeks

You can use the first half of Outcome by itself. For many goals this will be enough, like reserve infantry and some police tactical units. You'll get a significant amount of ruck training including back-to-backs along with focused work capacity sessions. Determine your need for Strength-Endurance training and swap in SE for one or both blocks of Fighter.

Week	Day 1	Day 2	Day 3	Day 4	Day 5	Day 6	Day 7
\multicolumn{8}{c}{OUTCOME/8 Weeks}							

Week	Day 1	Day 2	Day 3	Day 4	Day 5	Day 6	Day 7
1	FT	S/Ruck 2	LSS	FT	FK 5	Ruck 4	
2	FT	S/Ruck 2	LSS	FT	Peggy	Ruck 5	
3	FT	S/Ruck 2	LSS	FT		**Ruck 6**	**Ruck 4**
4	Deload	LSS		LSS		LSS	
5	**SE**	S/Ruck 4	LSS	**SE**	FK 5	Ruck 8	
6	**SE**	S/Ruck 4	LSS	**SE**	Peggy	Ruck 9	
7	**SE**	S/Ruck 4	LSS	**SE**		**Ruck 10**	**Ruck 6**
8	Deload	LSS		LSS		LSS	

Test for a 12-15 mile/35lb ruck benchmark at or near your target pace. Another way to use this is if your event is too far out to use Outcome's peaking block. Build your basic ruck proficiency and work capacity with this abbreviated variant and switch to a Continuation template. When you're a couple months out from your event, run the peaking portion of Outcome.

OUTCOME/12 Weeks

This abbreviated variant gives you a more advanced template with higher benchmarks and significant work capacity training. You get the two-a-days, enhanced SE training, and challenging back to back rucks. Good for light infantry, recce, and other specialized dismounted roles.

\multicolumn{8}{c}{OUTCOME / 12 Weeks}
Week	Day 1	Day 2	Day 3	Day 4	Day 5	Day 6	Day 7
1	FT	S/Ruck 2	LSS	FT	FK 5	Ruck 4	
2	FT	S/Ruck 2	LSS	FT	Peggy	Ruck 5	
3	FT	S/Ruck 2	LSS	FT		**Ruck 6**	**Ruck 4**
4	Deload	LSS		LSS		LSS	
5	FT	S/Ruck 4	LSS	FT	FK 5	Ruck 8	
6	FT	S/Ruck 4	LSS	FT	Peggy	Ruck 9	
7	FT	S/Ruck 4	LSS	FT		**Ruck 10**	**Ruck 6**
8	Deload	LSS		LSS		LSS	
\multicolumn{8}{c}{PEAK}
9	SE (LSS)	S/Ruck 6	SE (LSS)	MR 3-5	SE (LSS)	Ruck 12	
10	SE (LSS)	S/Ruck 6	SE (LSS)	Hill	SE (LSS)	Ruck 13	
11	SE (LSS)	S/Ruck 6	SE (LSS)		SE	**Ruck 14**	**Ruck 8**
12	Taper	LSS		LSS		LSS	

Add an additional recovery week (13) if tapering for an event or benchmark testing.

Test for a 15-18 mile ruck benchmark at or near target pace.

OUTCOME/ Experienced

If you have a strong ruck background start Outcome at a more suitable entry point. Adjust ruck loads accordingly.

	OUTCOME / Experienced						
5	FT	S/Ruck 4	LSS	FT	FK 5	Ruck 8	
6	FT	S/Ruck 4	LSS	FT	Peggy	Ruck 9	
7	FT	S/Ruck 4	LSS	FT		**Ruck 10**	**Ruck 6**
8	Deload	LSS		LSS		LSS	
			PEAK				
9	SE (LSS)	S/Ruck 6	SE (LSS)	MR 3-5	SE (LSS)	Ruck 12	
10	SE (LSS)	S/Ruck 6	SE (LSS)	Hill	SE (LSS)	Ruck 13	
11	SE (LSS)	S/Ruck 6	SE (LSS)		SE	**Ruck 14**	**Ruck 8**
12	Deload	LSS		LSS		LSS	
13	SE (LSS)	S/Ruck 8	SE (LSS)	MR 3-5	SE (LSS)	Ruck 16	
14	SE (LSS)	S/Ruck 8	SE (LSS)	Hill	SE (LSS)	Ruck 17	
15	SE (LSS)	S/Ruck 8	SE (LSS)		SE	**Ruck 18**	**Ruck 10**
16	Taper	LSS		LSS		LSS	
17		LSS		LSS		**Ruck 20**	

This is a good approach for someone already in a combat arms role that needs to brush up/peak for a challenging school or course.

PEAK

Peak can be detached from Outcome and used by itself leading up to selections/schools/events provided you have a suitable foundation in place. It can be used anytime you need to sharpen or ramp up operational fitness. Use just the first three weeks or the whole thing, based on your goals.

	OUTCOME/ Peaking Phase						
9	SE (LSS)	S/Ruck 6	SE (LSS)	MR 3-5	SE (LSS)	Ruck 12	
10	SE (LSS)	S/Ruck 6	SE (LSS)	Hill	SE (LSS)	Ruck 13	
11	SE (LSS)	S/Ruck 6	SE (LSS)		SE	**Ruck 14**	**Ruck 8**
12	Deload	LSS		LSS		LSS	
13	SE (LSS)	S/Ruck 8	SE (LSS)	MR 3-5	SE (LSS)	Ruck 16	
14	SE (LSS)	S/Ruck 8	SE (LSS)	Hill	SE (LSS)	Ruck 17	
15	SE (LSS)	S/Ruck 8	SE (LSS)		SE	**Ruck 18**	**Ruck 10**
16	Taper	LSS		LSS		LSS	
17		LSS		LSS		**Ruck 20**	

During Peak, speedwork can replace Hill sessions if more is needed.

The taper can be used to lead up to your event instead of the benchmark test.

NO SHORTCUTS

Abbreviated variants aren't shortcuts. Abbreviated templates are used to align with lower benchmarks, varying levels of experience, and differing objectives. They're not meant to be squeezed in before selection/school because you didn't spend enough time building your foundation leading up. An established infantry soldier using the experienced version of Outcome before a challenging school = good. Efficient use of time. A civilian or beginner squeezing Peak in before selection because he's short on time = bad.

CUSTOM

Outcome can be customized to include specialized fitness requirements like swimming. It can also be modified for minimal or no ruck work.

OUTCOME/ Amphibious

This is a sample template modified for swimming/water skills. Use it as a framework to incorporate your own specialized fitness requirements.

\multicolumn{8}{c}{OUTCOME/Amphibious}
Week	Day 1	Day 2	Day 3	Day 4	Day 5	Day 6	Day 7
1	FT	Swim	LSS	FT	FK 5	Ruck 4	
2	FT	Swim	LSS	FT	Peggy	Ruck 5	
3	FT	Swim	LSS	FT		Ruck 6	Ruck 4
4	Deload	LSS		LSS		LSS	
5	FT	Swim	LSS	FT	FK 5	Ruck 8	
6	FT	Swim	LSS	FT	Peggy	Ruck 9	
7	FT	Swim	LSS	FT		Ruck 10	Ruck 6
8	Deload	LSS		LSS		LSS	
\multicolumn{8}{c}{PEAK}
9	SE(LSS)	Swim	SE (LSS)	MR 3-5	SE (LSS)	Ruck 12	
10	SE(LSS)	Swim	SE (LSS)	Hill	SE (LSS)	Ruck 13	
11	SE(LSS)	Swim	SE (LSS)		SE	Ruck 14	Ruck 8
12	Deload	LSS		LSS		LSS	

13	SE(LSS)	**Swim**	SE (LSS)	MR 3-5	SE (LSS)	Ruck 16	
14	SE(LSS)	**Swim**	SE (LSS)	Hill	SE (LSS)	Ruck 17	
15	SE(LSS)	**Swim**	SE (LSS)		SE	**Ruck 18**	**Ruck 10**
16	Taper	LSS		LSS		LSS	
17		LSS		LSS		LSS	**Ruck 20**

Swimming is substituted for the Speed Ruck sessions in this example. If you need even more, swap out some of the two-a-day LSS runs during Peak. Do more or less as dictated by your needs/personal strengths/weaknesses.

I've left the ruck distances intact, but you might want to shorten them or cut them in half if the progression is too quick.

OUTCOME / No Ruck

This variant will be of interest to tactical law enforcement types or roles that don't require ruck specialization.

Simply transition from Velocity to the Outcome Peaking block. The first part of Outcome is primarily for building basic ruck proficiency and work capacity. You don't need it. You may not ruck much but you're still a load bearing animal: armor, breaching tools, secondary weapons, etc. So, during Peak ruck sessions are replaced with loaded work capacity training (Peggy, Weight Vest Runs), more speedwork, and more running in general. Equally important, you get the two-a-days and a concentrated strength-endurance phase. For you, Outcome becomes primarily a work capacity builder.

```
          ┌─────────┐
          │VELOCITY │
          └─────────┘
               ⬇
```

			PEAK				
9	SE (LSS)	Hill	SE (LSS)	MR 3-5	SE (LSS)	LR 12	
10	SE (LSS)	WVR	SE (LSS)	MR 3-5	SE (LSS)	LR 13	
11	SE (LSS)	Hill	SE (LSS)		SE	LR 14	Peggy
12	Deload	LSS		LSS		LSS	
13	SE (LSS)	Hill	SE (LSS)	MR 3-5	SE (LSS)	LR 16	
14	SE (LSS)	WVR	SE (LSS)	MR 3-5	SE (LSS)	LR 17	
15	SE (LSS)	Hill	SE (LSS)		SE	LR 18	Peggy
16	Taper	LSS		LSS		LSS	
17		LSS		LSS		LSS	

NOTES

MR: Mile Repeat 3-5 reps. Tempo Run can also be used.

WVR: Weight Vest Run 30-60 minutes

LSS: 60-120 Minute Run or 30-120 Minutes during two-a-days

LSS/Deload: 30-60 Minute Run. Other modes can be used – cycling, swimming, etc.

LSS/Taper: 30 Minute Run

LR: Long Run (miles)

Peggy: These sessions are going to be invaluable for selection prep and building work capacity. Peggy can be performed on Day 5 or 7 or swapped with the LR (Peggy on Day 6, LR on Day 7).

Hill: 30-120 minutes, any hill session: CHR, Vert Ladders, etc. Weight Vest Runs can also be used as an alternative.

OUTCOME / Minimal Ruck

A good fit for tactical law enforcement units that occasionally embed with military units or have a minor rural mandate.

Week	Day 1	Day 2	Day 3	Day 4	Day 5	Day 6	Day 7
\multicolumn{8}{c}{OUTCOME / Minimal Ruck}							
1	FT	Ruck 2	LSS	FT	Peggy	LR 4	
2	FT	WVR	LSS	FT	TPO 3-5	LR 5	
3	FT	Hill	LSS	FT		LR 6	Ruck 4
4	Deload	LSS		LSS		LSS	
5	FT	Ruck 4	LSS	FT	Peggy	LR 8	
6	FT	WVR	LSS	FT	TPO 3-5	LR 9	
7	FT	Hill	LSS	FT		LR 10	Ruck 6
8	Deload	LSS		LSS		LSS	
				PEAK			
9	SE (LSS)	Ruck 6	SE (LSS)	MR 3-5	SE (LSS)	LR 12	
10	SE (LSS)	WVR	SE (LSS)	MR 3-5	SE (LSS)	LR 13	
11	SE (LSS)	Hill	SE (LSS)		SE	LR 14	Ruck 8

12	Deload	LSS		LSS		LSS	
13	SE (LSS)	Ruck 8	SE (LSS)	MR 3-5	SE (LSS)	LR 16	
14	SE (LSS)	WVR	SE (LSS)	MR 3-5	SE (LSS)	LR 17	
15	SE (LSS)	Hill	SE (LSS)		SE	LR 18	Ruck 10
16	Taper	LSS		LSS		LSS	
17		LSS		LSS		LSS	

NOTES

WVR: Weight Vest Run. Hill training can be used instead.

Hill: Any hill session – CHR, Peggy, Vert Ladders, etc.

TPO: Tempo Run 3-5 miles. Add 1 mile warmup/cooldown.

Adjust for more or less rucking as needed.

PHYSICAL FITNESS TESTS

If you're in a process that includes periodic or entry level fitness tests (PFT), you can occasionally incorporate them in your training.

PFTs are relatively easy. Green Protocol will cover most if not all your bases. Use relevant exercises in your clusters, pay attention to pace during speedwork, and you won't have to do a bunch of extra PFT prep. You *will* need to prepare for any specialized fitness not covered in this program – like swimming or water skills.

Put PFTs somewhere near the end of deload weeks, preferably day 6 or 7:

OUTCOME							
Week	Day 1	Day 2	Day 3	Day 4	Day 5	Day 6	Day 7
1	FT	S/Ruck 2	LSS	FT	FK 5	Ruck 4	
2	FT	S/Ruck 2	LSS	FT	Peggy	Ruck 5	
3	FT	S/Ruck 2	LSS	FT		Ruck 6	Ruck 4
4	Deload	LSS		LSS		LSS	
5	FT	S/Ruck 4	LSS	FT	FK 5	Ruck 8	
6	FT	S/Ruck 4	LSS	FT	Peggy	Ruck 9	
7	FT	S/Ruck 4	LSS	FT		Ruck 10	Ruck 6
8	Deload	LSS		LSS		LSS	**PFT**

	PEAK						
9	SE (LSS)	S/Ruck 6	SE (LSS)	MR 3-5	SE (LSS)	Ruck 12	
10	SE (LSS)	S/Ruck 6	SE (LSS)	Hill	SE (LSS)	Ruck 13	
11	SE (LSS)	S/Ruck 6	SE (LSS)		SE	Ruck 14	Ruck 8
12	Deload	LSS		LSS		LSS	**PFT**
13	SE (LSS)	S/Ruck 8	SE (LSS)	MR 3-5	SE (LSS)	Ruck 16	
14	SE (LSS)	S/Ruck 8	SE (LSS)	Hill	SE (LSS)	Ruck 17	
15	SE (LSS)	S/Ruck 8	SE (LSS)		SE	Ruck 18	Ruck 10
16	Taper	LSS		LSS		LSS	
17		LSS		LSS		LSS	Ruck 20

I used Outcome in this example, but PFTs can be included in any template. Placing them somewhere near the beginning and end will give you a kind of progress report. Keep in mind where you place your PFT might skew the results. In the example above the first one is done during Week 8 – there's no structured SE leading up to it. Kill two birds and have it double as a test day for the upcoming SE phase. For the second PFT (Week 12), you'll have a solid three weeks of SE and two-a-days under your belt. Your results will likely reflect that.

You can use the results to tweak future training if needed. That might mean throwing in a few extra sets of pull-ups during SE or swapping out the occasional Hill Run for extra speedwork. Or doing a push-up finisher after Fighter in addition to including them in your Peggy cluster. Train consistently and make relevant choices when it comes to exercise selection, speedwork pacing, etc. By the time you complete Foundation, you won't have to do much, if any, extra PFT prep.

TRAIN HARD, FIGHT EASY

PFTs are usually the easiest part of any selection process. They're an initial sorting process to cut numbers and ensure candidates possess the bare minimum before the real work begins. Even so, there are two mistakes I see over and over again.

Mistake number 1 is training for the minimums.

Mistake number 2 is not taking fatigue from consecutive events into account.

You won't rise to the occasion. You'll fall to the level of your training.

It's one thing to stroll into the gym in the middle of the afternoon when you're well rested and fed, do a set of pull-ups, chat with your buddies for 10 minutes, strut over to the bench and hit the required weight. The sun is shining, conditions are ideal, and nothing is at stake. You hit the minimums, maybe exceed them. All is well in the world.

Contrast that with test day. You probably didn't sleep well. Testing is being held at some ungodly hour in the morning. It's still dark, maybe cold. You're on someone else's time. There will be nerves - a new career or dream team at stake. Maybe something you've been passionate about your entire life. You've been bragging to friends, family, co-workers, and total strangers that you're trying out for SWAT or whatever. Enter the weight of expectation and fear of failure.

The instructors aren't particularly friendly. Some of them are downright mean. They don't seem to recognize how special you are. You learn you'll be doing the events back to back with mere minutes between stations. In a different order than you're used to. Doing your best push-up set right after a heart pounding 1.5 mile run is a different beast. You grab some real estate and start pumping. The assessor counts '1…2….2…2…3'some of your reps are being disqualified because of poor form. You might have to hit 50 reps to earn 40 good ones. All good. Let's say you squeeze out the win - are you ready for pull-ups in the next 5 minutes? I came across a candidate that was unable to do a single pull-up after his Cooper's run. He claimed he was hitting 5 in training. I believed him. He didn't account for the fatigue of back-to-back events and test-day stress. And he trained for the bare minimum in ideal circumstances.

Train well beyond the minimums and mimic the conditions you'll face during the real thing. For example, if the minimum push-ups, pull-ups and 1.5 Mile are 40, 5, and 11 minutes, train until you can hit *at least* 60, 10, and 9:30. Then train so you can hit those numbers back to back with minimal rest in ANY order on your worst day. Think about how well prepared you'll feel knowing with absolute certainty that you can stop whatever you're doing at anytime and destroy it. A PFT should be a reflection or snapshot of your existing fitness. If you're training consistently and using a program like Green Protocol, you won't need to excessively target specific PFT numbers, they'll be a permanent part of your underlying ability. That said, there's absolutely nothing wrong with doing a little extra prep or shoring up weaknesses a few weeks before a meaningful PFT.

CONTINUATION

CONTINUATION

"People think focus means saying yes to the thing you've got to focus on. But that's not what it means at all. It means saying no the hundred other good ideas that there are. You have to pick carefully."

Steve Jobs

Capacity, Velocity, and Outcome are building templates. You're training harder than usual, more than usual. Everything else in your life takes a backseat. Temporary sacrifice for a permanent increase in ability. Additionally, Foundation is geared toward entry level fitness and special events like selection or schools, most of which tend to be endurance biased. After you get on a team, you may want to scale back on the endurance, depending on your role. You might find it more beneficial to put on muscle and slide a little bit closer on the spectrum toward strength and power. Continuation will give you that wriggle room to decide where you want to be now that you're left to your own devices.

At the end of the day your job isn't fitness. It's operations. Fitness is a single spoke on the wheel. You have to spend time on other job related skills like shooting, CQB, nav, etc. Like fitness, these are disciplines in and of themselves that can take a lifetime to master. Then there's the job itself which might include deployments, call-outs, and general disruption to your formerly predictable schedule. You won't always be able to stick to a strict by-the-book training program. You also (presumably) live in the real world which involves family, hobbies, holidays etc. You have to integrate your new cyborg level of fitness by adjusting your rate of progress to mesh with your availability.

During Continuation the focus shifts from building to performing or doing that which you've trained to do. Foundation is a warrior phase. Continuation is an operator phase.

Continuation has several objectives:

Free up time for other pursuits.

Free up energy for other pursuits.

Progress fitness at a sustainable tempo.

Continuation is not maintenance. Maintenance implies stagnation. Continuation is progression albeit at a slower pace.

CHANGING GEARS WITH CONTINUATION

Training tempo is reduced primarily through the following:

Using time instead of distance to program running/conditioning.

Training for 4-5 days/week instead of 6.

Both of these are options, not rules. They're meant to make your life easier if you need it. If you don't, you can continue to train six days a week and or use distance.

Distance based programming takes time, the less fit you are the more time it'll take. During Continuation, you can program using duration. Instead of a 10 mile run, run for 60-120 minutes. Like that. This gives you the flexibility to adjust your training week to align with your schedule and abilities.

The Continuation templates are presented as 6 day models, but guidelines will be provided for reducing that to 4-5 days. 5-6 days is ideal. 4 can be solid. 3's possible if you're doubling up and doing two-a-days.

There's no such thing as a free lunch. Freeing up that extra time comes at the expense of training volume and intensity. Which results in slower progress. It's a necessary trade-off unless you're unemployed or Bruce Wayne.

Several Continuation templates and models are provided. Choose the option that fits and modify as needed.

CONTINUATION MODELS

Hybrid

The Hybrid template is a simple but powerful approach that consist of nothing but strength training and running. Specialized training blocks (SE, hypertrophy, kettlebells etc.) can be inserted as needed. This is also a good fit if you get specific fitness like rucking or other skills from your day job, unit PT, sports etc. This one has several variants including the **Hybrid/Operator** template.

Concurrent/Combat Arms Template

C/CAT is a classic Green Protocol applied to combat fitness. All relevant sessions are trained on a weekly basis: strength, speedwork, elevation, rucking, and long easy endurance work. It keeps your skills sharp across the board. The best practice is to couple C/CAT with Capacity. Run Capacity for a block, followed by C/CAT, repeat. Capacity acts as base training and keeps your foundational strength and conditioning topped off. Then that general strength and conditioning gets channeled into C/CAT and converted into specific fitness. The ratio of Capacity : C/CAT can be adjusted as needed. Capacity becomes base, C/CAT becomes specificity.

Integrated/Combat Arms Template

I/CAT is essentially a compressed version of Capacity/Velocity/Outcome that can be repeated indefinitely. It's a periodized template that covers all bases. A good fit for those with a relatively predictable schedule that want a linear approach.

Block Training

Block Training isn't a template, it's a backup plan. Block Training is used when your schedule gets disrupted, and you experience frequent changes in training environment. You have access to a gym for a few weeks, and then you don't. BT involves categorizing fitness into 3 week blocks based on the equipment you have and doing those blocks when fortune forces your hand. When you have access to barbells, hit the weights hard and do a max-strength or hypertrophy block. When you're shunted out in the middle of nowhere with only your carcass and a dumbbell, switch to SE/Green. Like that.

Mike India

AKA the Missing Ingredient approach. Add only what is missing. This is for you if you have a busy life with plenty of physical activity. For example, you have mandatory unit PT every morning, train a sport in the evenings, and have a fairly active day job. Adding a full blown strength & conditioning protocol on top of that might be unsustainable and counterproductive. Mike India is a strategy for adding the training component(s) you don't get from other activities.

LONG TERM PROGRAMMING - BASELINE/DETOUR

This applies to all of the Continuation templates.

The baseline/detour approach is a simple long term planning strategy for operational athletes. We're not seasonal competitors with fixed/scheduled events.

It works like this. Pick a Continuation template that bests suits your lifestyle and goals. This will be the program you use most of the year, your baseline program. This should be a program that pays the bills. If you're a high speed recce guy, Zulu/HT or Mass Protocol wouldn't be your baseline template. C/CAT or Hybrid make a little more sense.

After establishing your baseline, take training detours as needed. Detours might include doing a few blocks of mass building, training for a specific event like an ultramarathon, or tweaking your fitness a few weeks prior to PFT. You'll deviate from your baseline program, do the training required for the new objective, and return to baseline when complete.

Baseline/Detour examples will be provided for each Continuation template. It'll give you food for thought and ideas on how to play to each templates strengths and weaknesses.

HYBRID, HYBRID/OP

Just lifting and running. No clutter. Simple, focused, and powerful. Very flexible. If and when you need to work on other areas, throw in a specialized training block. The Hybrid acts as your baseline program. Take training detours as needed. It's also a good choice if you get specialized fitness through unit PT, sports, and hobbies. Use your personal time to focus on advancing the basics. If you need a booster shot of specific training like SE or rucking, do a SE block, Outcome, or whatever you need. Perpetually improving strength and endurance by way of running and lifting will build a solid base which you can transfer to any physical activity. There are two main versions of this template, the Hybrid or standard Hybrid, and Hybrid/Operator.

Hybrid/Op resembles Capacity in that it's a 50/50 split between running and lifting. Unlike Capacity it includes hill training and speedwork which allows it to be run indefinitely.

Regular **Hybrid** uses a two pronged approach. The first half emphasizes strength, the second running. During the strength phase favor your lifting sessions. This is the time for extra sets, building muscle, and spending time in the gym. Keep the running manageable. This isn't the best time to do a 25 mile Long Run or 2 hours of Peggy's Hills. 'Manageable' varies based on the individual, but you get the idea. If running is interfering with the primary goal of building strength, you're doing it wrong. Operator (any version) is the recommended strength program.

During the second phase, pivot. Prioritize running. Go nuts. Extend the length/duration/rounds etc. Push the envelope. Train for an ultra if you want. Or keep it reasonable. For some, a Long Run might be 30 miles. For others, an hour. Your goals and lifestyle will dictate. Fighter template is recommended for the lifting component.

What makes this protocol especially effective is the built in periodization. Each phase complements the other. During the lifting phase, you back off the running which gives your body a break from the particular stressors that brings. When you step on the gas and ramp up the mileage, you back off the frequent heavy lifting and the stressors *that* brings. Lifting benefits running, running benefits lifting, and cycling between lower and higher volume of both ensures longevity and maximal results.

Read the **Modifications** section carefully, this is a flexible template with a few different variations. One of them might be your perfect program.

HYBRID

HYBRID							
Week	Day 1	Day 2	Day 3	Day 4	Day 5	Day 6	Day 7
1	OP	Hill	OP	LSS	OP	LR	
2	OP	Speed	OP	LSS	OP	LR	
3	OP	Hill	OP	LSS	OP	LR	
4	OP	Speed	OP	LSS	OP	LR	
5	OP	Hill	OP	LSS	OP	LR	
6	OP	Speed	OP	LSS	OP	LR	
7				Deload			
8	FT	Hill	LSS	FT	Speed	FK	
9	FT	Hill	LSS	FT	Speed	LR	
10	FT	Hill	LSS	FT	Speed	FK	
11	FT	Hill	LSS	FT	Speed	LR	
12	FT	Hill	LSS	FT	Speed	FK	
13	FT	Hill	LSS	FT	Speed	LR	
14				Deload			

NOTES

During the OPERATOR phase LSS can replace any or all Hill or Speed sessions.

OP = Any Operator variant

FT = Fighter template

LSS = LSS jogging 30-120 minutes. Distance/miles/kms can also be used. During Continuation other forms of LSS can be used, cycling, swimming, jump rope etc. Best practice for operational athletes is to run for most sessions but occasionally supplementing with other modes is acceptable.

Extra LSS sessions can be done on OP or FT days.

FK = Fartlek. Program using distance or duration.

LR = Long Run. Program using distance or duration.

Speed = Any speed session (Mile Repeats, Tempo, 400M Repeats etc.). HICs from Tactical Barbell II, or any HIIT/Metcon style workout can also be used.

Hill = Hill Runs, Peggy's Hills, or any hill training. Hill work from Tactical Barbell II can be used here. Peggy's Hills, Apex, Bloody Lungs, etc. are all great ways to incorporate SE and work capacity.

This is Continuation, so customize and fiddle around with the parts to suit your needs. Program LSS/LR by time, distance, or a mix of both. Adjust the number of training days per week as needed. For example, during the Fighter/second half of the template drop the LSS session for the week. You Can also change the type of session you drop week-to-week or based on strengths/weaknesses. This gives you an effective well-rounded 5 day program. During the Operator phase you can do one or more of the conditioning sessions on your lifting days if that suits your schedule. Better to be consistent with less than inconsistent with more.

Get creative. Hill and Speed/HIC sessions are a perfect way to sneak in some SE and work capacity if needed. Peggy's Hills is an incredible SE and general work capacity session. On Speed/HIC days use GCs (General Conditioning HICs) from *Tactical Barbell II* for even more mixed modality conditioning. A good approach is to keep the GC style conditioning for Operator phases and use the running based speed/HICs for Fighter. Adjust accordingly for your goals.

Keep to the spirit of the template. During the Operator phase, emphasize strength. This is the time to do extra sets, squeeze in GCs, and push it in the gym. Keep the conditioning sessions manageable. When it's time to prioritize running, start extending the limits in that area and allow lifting to take a temporary backseat. Stick with a minimal cluster. Don't try and break records in the gym. This is where you get to experiment with endurance beyond your comfort zone. Individual work capacity varies, so this will mean different things to different people. This is an incredibly effective and enjoyable form of training. It prevents staleness and ensures continuous improvement in both strength and endurance.

SAMPLE PREFILLED HYBRID

This is an example only. I encourage you to create your own. Your version might look very different.

Week	Day 1	Day 2	Day 3	Day 4	Day 5	Day 6	Day 7
\multicolumn{8}{c}{**HYBRID**}							
1	OP	30-60	OP	30-60	OP	60-90	
2	OP	30-60	OP	30-60	OP	60-90	
3	OP	30	OP	30	OP	60-90	
4	OP	400/6	OP	30-60	OP	60-90	
5	OP	400/8	OP	30-60	OP	60-90	
6	OP	400/10	OP	30-60	OP	60-90	
7				Deload			
8	FT	Peggy	60-90	FT	MR 3-5	90-120	
9	FT	CHR	60-90	FT	TPO 3-5	90-120	
10	FT	Peggy	60-90	FT	MR 3-5	90-120	
11	FT	CHR	60-90	FT	TPO 3-5	90-120	
12	FT	Peggy	60-90	FT	MR 3-5	90-120	
13	FT	CHR	60-90	FT	TPO 3-5	90-120	
14				Deload			

NOTES

LSS: Prescribed in minutes

FK: Prescribed in minutes

LR: Prescribed in minutes

MR: Mile Repeats (miles)

TPO: Tempo Run (miles). Add 1 mile warm-up/1 mile cooldown jog

Peggy: 30-120 minutes

CHR: Continuous Hill Run 30-120 minutes

In this example I use a mix of time and distance for the conditioning sessions to give you some food for thought. You can use just one or the other if desired.

REDUCED TRAINING WEEKS

Sample five day Fighter phase. For Operator phase LSS can be done before or after lifting sessions to cut down on days.

\multicolumn{8}{c}{HYBRID}						
Week	Day 1	Day 2	Day 3	Day 4	Day 5	Day 6	Day 7
1	OP	LSS	OP	LSS	OP	LR	
2	OP	LSS	OP	LSS	OP	LR	
3	OP	LSS	OP	LSS	OP	LR	
4	OP	Hill	OP	LSS	OP	LR	
5	OP	Speed	OP	LSS	OP	LR	
6	OP	Hill	OP	LSS	OP	LR	
7				Deload			
8	FT	Speed	LSS	FT		LR	
9	FT	Hill	LSS	FT		LR	
10	FT	Speed	LSS	FT		LR	
11	FT	Hill	LSS	FT		LR	
12	FT	Speed	LSS	FT		LR	
13	FT	Hill	LSS	FT		LR	
14				Deload			

The 4 day below is a good fit if you're strapped for time. If you're a recreational trainee without occupational fitness requirements, it layers over top of a busy schedule fairly well:

Week	Day 1	Day 2	Day 3	Day 4	Day 5	Day 6	Day 7
\multicolumn{8}{c}{**HYBRID**}							
1	OP	LSS	OP	LSS	OP	LR	
2	OP	LSS	OP	LSS	OP	LR	
3	OP	LSS	OP	LSS	OP	LR	
4	OP	LSS	OP	LSS	OP	LR	
5	OP	LSS	OP	LSS	OP	LR	
6	OP	LSS	OP	LSS	OP	LR	
7				Deload			
8	FT	Speed		FT		LR	
9	FT	Hill		FT		LR	
10	FT	Speed		FT		LR	
11	FT	Hill		FT		LR	
12	FT	Speed		FT		LR	
13	FT	Hill		FT		LR	
14				Deload			

MODIFICATIONS

ABBREVIATED

The abbreviated variant is useful when more training flexibility is needed. Good for those with unpredictable schedules (frequent deployment, field exercises, etc.) that can't commit to a 12 week cycle.

\multicolumn{8}{c}{**HYBRID/Abbreviated**}

Week	Day 1	Day 2	Day 3	Day 4	Day 5	Day 6	Day 7
1	OP	Speed	OP	LSS	OP	LR	
2	OP	Hill	OP	LSS	OP	LR	
3	OP	Speed	OP	LSS	OP	LR	
4	FT	Hill	LSS	FT	Speed	LR	
5	FT	Hill	LSS	FT	Speed	LR	
6	FT	Hill	LSS	FT	Speed	LR	
7				Deload			

STRENGTH EMPHASIS

More lifting. With this one you're using a longer Operator phase. More lifting overall and you get the benefits of a brief advanced running block at the end of the cycle.

Week	Day 1	Day 2	Day 3	Day 4	Day 5	Day 6	Day 7
			HYBRID/Strength Emphasis				
1	OP	Hill	OP	LSS	OP	LR	
2	OP	Speed	OP	LSS	OP	LR	
3	OP	Hill	OP	LSS	OP	LR	
4	OP	Speed	OP	LSS	OP	LR	
5	OP	Hill	OP	LSS	OP	LR	
6	OP	Speed	OP	LSS	OP	LR	
7				Deload			
8	FT	Hill	LSS	FT	Speed	LR	
9	FT	Hill	LSS	FT	Speed	LR	
10	FT	Hill	LSS	FT	Speed	LR	
11				Deload			

CONDITIONING EMPHASIS

More emphasis on running/conditioning. For those that primarily use the Fighter/Green approach but could do with a little extra strength training on a regular basis.

HYBRID / Conditioning Emphasis								
Week	Day 1	Day 2	Day 3	Day 4	Day 5	Day 6	Day 7
1	OP	Hill	OP	LSS	OP	LR	
2	OP	Speed	OP	LSS	OP	LR	
3	OP	Hill	OP	LSS	OP	LR	
Deload							
5	FT	Hill	LSS	FT	Speed	LR	
6	FT	Hill	LSS	FT	Speed	LR	
7	FT	Hill	LSS	FT	Speed	LR	
8	FT	Hill	LSS	FT	Speed	LR	
9	FT	Hill	LSS	FT	Speed	LR	
10	FT	Hill	LSS	FT	Speed	LR	
Deload							

HYBRID/OPERATOR

Hybrid/Op is a 50/50 split. The Fighter phase is dropped. Good fit for police special operations or similar roles that don't have an extensive endurance component.

Week	Day 1	Day 2	Day 3	Day 4	Day 5	Day 6	Day 7
\multicolumn{8}{c}{HYBRID/Op}
1	OP	Hill	OP	LSS	OP	FK	
2	OP	Speed	OP	LSS	OP	LR	
3	OP	Hill	OP	LSS	OP	FK	
4	OP	Speed	OP	LSS	OP	LR	
5	OP	Hill	OP	LSS	OP	FK	
6	OP	Speed	OP	LSS	OP	LR	
Deload							

Turning this into a 5 day template is a little trickier because it's meant to be a 50/50 split, but it can be done. Do the LSS after an Operator session. Or keep it on day 4 but do the bare minimum 30 minutes. You can also turn this into a 3-4 day template using an AM/PM split. Lift in the AM, run in the PM, or vice versa.

BASELINE/DETOUR

The Hybrid is a perfect fit for the Baseline/Detour approach because it keeps the basics covered at all times. Here's an example of a what an idealized year of baseline training might look like:

Base/Capacity	Hybrid	Hybrid	Hybrid
8 weeks	14 weeks	14 weeks	14 weeks

Start the year with Base Building or Capacity. Any version. There's a lot of flex here. Use the hypertrophy variant of Capacity to get mass building in at the beginning of the year or use classic TB Base Building for SE and 'under armor' strengthening.

Here's what a long term approach might look like with training detours:

Base	Mass	Hybrid	Crossfit	Hybrid
8 weeks	12 weeks	14 weeks	3 weeks	14 weeks

In this example the trainee included 12 weeks of hypertrophy training at the beginning of the year. Later in the year he added three weeks of Crossfit for general work capacity training and novelty.

There's no limit to how long a training detour might take. You might decide to drop everything for a year or two while you pursue a very specialized goal like competitive strongman or an ultramarathon.

Life has a way of disrupting long term plans so don't get too attached to a pretty 52 week schedule. Use the baseline/detour approach as a guide rather than a carved in stone path. The guiding principle is to spend the most time on domains and protocols that pay the bills. Take occasional detours to shore up weaknesses or add novelty. If you're a high speed operational athlete, spending 80% of the year on hypertrophy doesn't make a whole lot of sense.

CONCURRENT/
Combat Arms Template

C/CAT as the name suggests is a concurrent approach. All the primary combat arms domains are trained on a weekly basis. In addition to being an extremely effective standalone template, C/CAT can be used as a placeholder. If you're coming off Foundation and have a few months to kill before a school or event, C/CAT will keep your skills sharp and progressing in the right direction. Switch to the Outcome peaking block before the event. Good to go.

If you don't ruck for a living take an extra day off or sub in something relevant; SE, (a la Fighter/Bangkok), swimming, Weight Vest Run, GC sessions, etc.

The sessions can be rearranged but keep Fighter spread throughout the week. No more than three days between Fighter sessions is best practice to avoid a detraining effect. The Long Run is usually done at the end of the week on Day 6 or 7, but that's not carved a must.

C/CAT works especially well when combined with Capacity. Run Capacity first as a foundation builder, follow it up with a block or two of C/CAT, rinse, repeat. Change up the ratio of Capacity : C/CAT as required. Use the 8 week version of Capacity to keep your blocks tighter.

C/CAT								
Week	Day 1	Day 2	Day 3	Day 4	Day 5	Day 6	Day 7
1	FT	Speed	LSS	FT		Ruck	LR
2	FT	Hill	LSS	FT		Ruck	FK
3	FT	Speed	LSS	FT		Ruck	LR
4	FT	Hill	LSS	FT		Ruck	FK
5	FT	Speed	LSS	FT		Ruck	LR
6	FT	Hill	LSS	FT		Ruck	FK
Deload								
8	SE	Speed	LSS	SE		Ruck	LR
9	SE	Hill	LSS	SE		Ruck	FK
10	SE	Speed	LSS	SE		Ruck	LR
Deload								

NOTES

The example above is six days/week. Sessions can be dropped to make it 4-5 days some or all of the time. Alternate the dropped session (i.e., ruck one week, LSS another, etc.) or choose based on needs/strengths/weaknesses. For example, some find rucking every other week sufficient. Don't drop the Long Run, Fighter, or SE when reducing weekly training.

FT: Fighter Template

Ruck: Ruck or Speed Ruck. Other sessions can be substituted: Swimming, LSS, etc. Can also be used as an extra day off.

LSS/LR/FK: Can be programmed using duration or distance.

Speed/HIC: Speedwork, High Intensity Conditioning sessions (*Tactical Barbell II*), or any Metcon/HIIT style training.

Hill: Continuous Hill Run, Peggy's Hills, Hill sessions from *Tactical Barbell II* or other sources.

BASELINE/DETOUR

A good practice is to combine C/CAT with Capacity. Capacity builds general strength and fitness, C/CAT converts that general strength and fitness into specific conditioning for the combat arms soldier. Use an 8 week Capacity block to keep your programming tighter. Sample approaches:

Capacity	C/CAT	Capacity	C/CAT	Capacity	C/CAT
8 weeks	10 weeks	8 weeks	10 weeks	8 weeks	10 weeks

You can adjust the ratio of Capacity : C/CAT as needed. In the example below more time is spent on Capacity. This trainee wants to build a bigger wider base, before specializing with C/CAT. He uses 12 week Capacity blocks:

Capacity	C/CAT	Capacity	C/CAT	Capacity	C/CAT
12 weeks	10 weeks	12 weeks	10 weeks	12 weeks	10 weeks

With a few detours:

Hypertrophy	Capacity (H)	C/CAT	C/CAT	Outcome/Peak
12 weeks	12 weeks	10 weeks	10 weeks	8 weeks

This trainee spends the first part of the year building mass. The hypertrophy (H) version of Capacity is used to align with the focus on muscle building and creates a smooth transition to increased conditioning. Then on to C/CAT for specific operational fitness. Fortune interferes - the trainee gets an unexpected last minute opportunity to attend a challenging school. He has a limited amount of time to prepare, and transitions to the Outcome/peak phase prior to attendance.

INTEGRATED/
Combat Arms Template

I/CAT is essentially Capacity, Velocity, and Outcome compressed into a single template. I/CAT works well for those that have a relatively predictable schedule and want a comprehensive, repeatable training plan that focuses on all the domains/skills relevant to combat fitness. I/CAT is a good fit for reservists and guard units.

I/CAT employs a loose form of linear/block periodization utilizing the 'ideal' order of operations. It starts with hypertrophy and transitions to maximal-strength. Maximal-strength tapers off and running/conditioning increases. I/CAT ends with specificity: rucking, muscular-endurance, and general work capacity.

\multicolumn{8}{c}{**I/CAT**}							
Week	Day 1	Day 2	Day 3	Day 4	Day 5	Day 6	Day 7
1	Zulu	Zulu		Zulu	Zulu		
2	Zulu	Zulu		Zulu	Zulu		
3	Zulu	Zulu		Zulu	Zulu		
4	Deload						
5	OP	Speed	OP	LSS	OP	LR	
6	OP	Hill	OP	LSS	OP	Ruck*	
7	OP	Speed	OP	LSS	OP	LR	
8	Deload						
9	FT	Hill	LSS	FT	LSS	LR	
10	FT	Speed	LSS	FT	LSS	Ruck*	
11	FT	Hill	LSS	FT		LR	
12	Deload						
13	SE	Speed	SE	LSS	SE	LR	
14	SE	Hill	SE	LSS	SE	Ruck*	
15	SE	Speed	SE	LSS	SE	LR	

*Other sessions can be substituted as required: Long Runs, Swimming, additional SE, etc.

NOTES

Zulu: Zulu/HT, Tactical Barbell's *Mass Protocol*, or any other hypertrophy/muscle building plan can be used. You're not restricted to a four day plan. Do more or less as desired. Keep conditioning minimal during hypertrophy phase. No more than 2-3 brief HIIT/HIC/METCON style sessions, or 20-30 minutes of easy LSS running/cycling/swimming etc.

OP: Any Operator variant/any strength template.

LSS: Program for distance or time. For operational athletes most sessions should be running, but other modalities can be used to supplement.

Hill: Any Hill session or loaded work. Continuous Hill Runs, Peggy, WVRs, Hill sessions from *Tactical Barbell II* or other sources.

LR: Long Run. Can be done for distance or time. Fartlek can also be used.

SE: Strength Endurance. Two or three day model.

Speed/HIC: Speed sessions, HICs from *Tactical Barbell II*, HIIT/Metcon style training from other sources.

Ruck: Other training can be substituted: Long Runs, Swimming, SE/GC/HIC, Weight Vest Run, etc.

BASELINE/DETOURS

I/CAT is a compressed version of CAT, so most of the detours you might take with a less inclusive template are already built-in.

Base Building (*Tactical Barbell II*) is a natural fit and can be incorporated once or twice a year. It acts as a general preparation phase for the substantive training. Capacity can be used instead of Base.

Base Building	I/CAT	Base Building	I/CAT
8 Weeks	15 Weeks	8 Weeks	15 Weeks

As far as other detours go, drop I/CAT, and do the new thing. When it's time to return to baseline, start a new I/CAT cycle.

Base Building	I/CAT	Kettlebells	I/CAT	No Ruck/Peak
8 Weeks	15 Weeks	8 Weeks	12 Weeks	3 Weeks

In this example a law enforcement member and army reservist starts her training year off with standard Tactical Barbell Base Building before transitioning to her go-to template, I/CAT. She comes across a kettlebell program that catches her eye and takes a detour. After returning to baseline (I/CAT) she's presented with an opportunity to select as a dog handler with her agency. She has a solid foundation in place but decides to give her running, SE, and work capacity a booster shot prior to the course. She drops the last three weeks of I/CAT due to time constraints and swaps in 3 weeks of Peaking using the Outcome/No-Ruck model. When the course rolls around, she's in top form and ready to go.

BLOCK TRAINING

Block Training is used when long term scheduling and access to equipment are disrupted or become unpredictable. It can also be used as standard programming by experienced trainees that hate long-term structure, aren't tied to linear progress, and/or have a nomadic lifestyle. I don't recommend it as standard programming for beginners. It's best to build up a solid level of baseline fitness before getting this random. That said, every operational athlete regardless of ability can use this approach as a backup plan if deployed to an environment with limited or no equipment.

A scenario that frequently arises is this:

'Just found out I'm travelling to Fantasia next week. I won't have access to barbells. I'll have three dumbbells, half a treadmill, and a pull-up bar. Can someone show me how to do Operator template with what I have?'

Instead of trying to do a half-assed strength training plan get in some high-quality SE/Endurance work. Fortune is giving you the opportunity to focus on a different objective, probably an objective you don't enjoy (does anyone like SE?). Adapt, seize it. Create an SE cluster using your bodyweight and the equipment you have. Add endurance based running for conditioning. Become a Green machine. When you return to the land of barbells, go back to an *effective* strength or hypertrophy protocol. Here's how it works.

During periods of uncertainty or sporadic mobility, break your training down into 2 or 3 simple blocks. For example:

Hypertrophy Block (Mass): Zulu/HT or MASS Protocol + conditioning

Strength Block (Black): Operator, Operator/DUP, or standard Zulu + conditioning

Endurance Block (Green): SE + Endurance based conditioning

Each block is 3 weeks in length. I've used *Tactical Barbell* terminology to label them so you can align them with existing TB protocols. Pair the strength domain with the appropriate type and volume of conditioning. You shouldn't be doing high volume endurance work with Mass. Choose the block you're going to run based on what you have available.

Do strength or hypertrophy blocks when you have access to barbells. Do endurance when equipment is limited or non-existent. Switch up between them as the situation dictates.

For example, you currently have access to a fully stocked gym. In a couple months you're deploying, and your equipment will consist of your body, running shoes, and maybe a few kettlebells. Knowing this in advance, you work on bulking up and getting strong while you have the barbells. You run nothing but strength and hypertrophy blocks leading up. Once deployed, you go Green. Create a bodyweight/kettlebell cluster for SE. Do things like hill training, speedwork & distance running for conditioning. Run the 3 week Green block on repeat until the situation changes. Partway through deployment, you go on leave and once again have access to barbells and Gucci equipment. You take advantage of it and transition to a three week hypertrophy block to pack some weight on. When you get back, you're shuttled between various FOBs and bases, with varying degrees of quality when it comes to training equipment. Switch up blocks accordingly.

Here's what a sample strength or Black block might look like:

BLACK							
Week	Day 1	Day 2	Day 3	Day 4	Day 5	Day 6	Day7
1	OP	HILL	OP	Speed/HIC	OP	LR	
2	OP	HILL	OP	Speed/HIC	OP	LR	
3	OP	HILL	OP	Speed/HIC	OP	LR	

Strength is prioritized. Distances, number of rounds, and duration for conditioning sessions should reflect that. HIC stands for High Intensity Conditioning and is a Tactical Barbell term for shorter duration/higher intensity training. Speedwork, Hill sprints, Metcon or HIIT style workouts fall under the HIC umbrella. The **Hybrid/Op** template can be used here as well.

Mass or hypertrophy block:

MASS							
Week	Day 1	Day 2	Day 3	Day 4	Day 5	Day 6	Day7
1	Zulu	Zulu	HIC	Zulu	Zulu	HIC	
2	Zulu	Zulu	HIC	Zulu	Zulu	HIC	
3	Zulu	Zulu	HIC	Zulu	Zulu	HIC	

This Mass block consists of Zulu/HT alongside HICs or speedwork.

Endurance block:

\multicolumn{8}{c}{GREEN}
Week	Day 1	Day 2	Day 3	Day 4	Day 5	Day 6	Day7
1	SE	LSS	Hill	SE	LSS		LR
2	SE	LSS	Speed	SE	LSS		LR
3	SE	LSS	Hill	SE	LSS		LR

SE training can be two or three days, all bodyweight, with equipment, or a mix. Because endurance is prioritized, conditioning sessions should be relatively long/high volume. For example, use speedwork sessions that are applicable to endurance work - Tempo Runs, Mile Repeats, 800M Repeats, rather than 100 meter sprints. The number of weekly conditioning sessions can be increased/decreased, and two-a-days can be incorporated.

NOTES

Block Training should generally be reserved for periods of frequent mobility and unpredictability. When things settle down or go back to 'normal' the best practice is to switch to a Continuation template/return to baseline.

That said, Block Training can be used by experienced trainees as standard programming. If you get bored sticking to one routine for long this might be the answer. Change blocks at random or based on a loose plan. I don't recommend this approach for beginners. If you're in the early stages of building your fitness, Block Training should only be used out of necessity.

How you approach Block Training is entirely up to you. Blocks can be run for longer than three weeks. String together as many as the situation dictates and roll with it. Customize the number/type of strength and conditioning sessions as necessary.

All of the existing Tactical Barbell protocols and individual training sessions can be used for Block Training. For more information on individual TB strength and conditioning sessions read *Tactical Barbell I: Strength* and *Tactical Barbell II: Conditioning*.

There is no baseline/detour approach with Block Training. This one by it's very nature doesn't include long term planning. You're thinking one or two blocks ahead at a time, or whatever's suitable for your immediate situation.

MIKE INDIA

The Missing Ingredient approach is an option for those that have pre-existing training or work that interferes with taking on a full blown strength and conditioning protocol. In many SOF or police units members are left to their own devices. In more conventional units that may not be the case. On top of any mandatory PT, you might be doing additional training on your own like MMA or other sports.

Mike India consists of adding ONLY the missing ingredient(s).

Here's an example using our favorite infantry soldier Private Bloggins. Bloggins has unit PT five days a week. It consists of the typical long runs, intervals, rucking, and some bodyweight stuff like push-ups, pull-ups, sit-ups etc.

What's missing?

Bloggins gets plenty of general endurance based conditioning. He gets a fair amount of strength-endurance. What he doesn't get is structured maximal-strength and hypertrophy training. He decides to give his SE a little extra love too, so he looks like a stud come PFT.

Based on that, Bloggins decides to spend his personal training time on the strength domains. He'll start with hypertrophy, transition to maximal-strength, finish with SE, rinse, repeat. (See the NERD STUFF: Order of Operations section in the Session Guide).

	Day 1	Day 2	Day 3	Day 4	Day 5	Day 6	Day 7
AM	Unit PT	Unit PT	Unit PT	Unit PT	Unit PT		
PM	H	H		H	H		

The above is what a week of Hypertrophy training (Zulu/HT) looks like for Bloggins. PT in the mornings, lifting in the evenings. He does hypertrophy for 6 weeks then transitions to Maximal-Strength. He uses Operator for his MS work:

	Day 1	Day 2	Day 3	Day 4	Day 5	Day 6	Day 7
AM	Unit PT	Unit PT	Unit PT	Unit PT	Unit PT		
PM	MS		MS		MS	Peggy	

He loves Peggy's Hills and decides to include it on the weekends just because. If he's tired or has a busy weekend planned, he can ditch it. Alternatively, he can add extra conditioning sessions to his free evenings if unit PT gets cancelled or he has extra energy.

Bloggins ends up doing 9 weeks of strength training with Operator. After that, he transitions to a 3 week SE block leading up to a periodic PF test:

	Day 1	Day 2	Day 3	Day 4	Day 5	Day 6	Day 7
AM	Unit PT	Unit PT	Unit PT	Unit PT	Unit PT		
PM	SE	Tempo	SE		SE		LR

He uses the 3-Day SE model and ramps up his conditioning slightly. He wants to destroy the 1.5 mile run this year, so he adds speedwork and a Long Run. His SE cluster consists of the exercises he'll be tested on.

BLOGGINS WANTS MORE CONDITIONING

Bloggins wants to ramp up his conditioning for a recce course. He cuts the lifting down to two days/week with Fighter template. This frees him up to do extra conditioning on his own time:

	Day 1	Day 2	Day 3	Day 4	Day 5	Day 6	Day 7
AM	Unit PT	Unit PT	Unit PT	Unit PT	Unit PT		
PM	FT	Tempo		FT	LSS		Peggy

BLOGGINS DOES MMA

Here's an example using MMA or any other sport in addition to Unit PT:

	Day 1	Day 2	Day 3	Day 4	Day 5	Day 6	Day 7
AM	Unit PT	Unit PT	Unit PT	Unit PT	Unit PT		
PM	MMA		MMA			MMA	

Bloggins looks at his busy training schedule and asks The Question:

What's missing?

He gets plenty of general conditioning through unit PT, which includes the usual Fun-Runs, intervals, and ruck marches. His MMA classes provide additional sport-specific conditioning.

Strength-Endurance? Unit PT sometimes includes calisthenics, push-ups, pull-ups, and sit-ups. MMA classes provide Bloggins with sport specific SE: pads, bag work, sparring/rolling, shadow boxing/combo drills. His SE is good to go. He doesn't need more.

Structured strength and hypertrophy training are the only major missing ingredients. Bloggins isn't overly concerned with hypertrophy. It's not a priority and he knows he'll get enough by way of maximal-strength training. He's narrowed his missing ingredient list down to strength.

Now it's time to determine the dose.

It makes little sense for Bloggins to add a four day balls-to-the-wall strength program with full-bore accessory work. He wants to be a better fighter, not a better lifter. The two day Fighter template is perfect for his situation.

The ability to sustain your training long term and make consistent progress is far more important than blowing your load after a week because you want to bench press 600lbs, win a triathlon, and become an ultimate fighting championship champion all at the same time. Be smart. Start with the minimum and add extra down the road when you can handle it. Here's Bloggins new schedule:

	Day 1	Day 2	Day 3	Day 4	Day 5	Day 6	Day 7
AM	Unit PT	Unit PT	Unit PT	Unit PT	Unit PT		
PM	MMA	FT	MMA		FT	MMA	

Deceptively simple. All he's done is add two days of strength training. That strength training will seep into all of his activities and multiply his results. It's a manageable schedule that he can run indefinitely without burning out. A slight tweak that'll pay off massively in the long run.

NOTES

Determine what's missing.

Determine the dose.

Start conservatively. Add more in small chunks over time if needed.

MIKE INDIA + FOUNDATION?

This one's mostly for the active duty readers but applies to anyone in a similar situation. Can you add Foundation using a Mike India approach? You can.

Do the Foundation sessions in the evenings or whenever you're left to your own devices.

Use the Modifications to make it possible. Use the templates in Easy Mode, abbreviate them, or aim for lower benchmarks if the standard progressions are too much in conjunction with unit PT or daily duties. Stick with session minimums when that option's available. Treat any Unit PT sessions that have a similar training effect as Foundation sessions to lower the workload.

It might take a little resource management, but it's very doable. Be realistic about your personal work capacity and what you can handle. Start conservative, add more as needed over time.

CH

'Just Do it' – **Nike**

I never truly appreciated Nike's slogan. I always wrote it off as being an overly simplistic slick catchphrase. Now I get it. It's a principle that's a little more fleshed out in my-favorite-training-book-of-all-time. My favorite training book isn't actually a training book at all. It's called the 'War of Art' by Steven Pressfield. The very first section to be exact, titled 'What I Do'. The 'secret' to being successful with training and pretty much anything else is contained in that 3 page section. It's probably more important than any fitness book (including this one) you'll ever pick up. The rest of 'War' you may or may not find useful.

A few parting thoughts and reminders. Motivation is for amateurs. Discipline is for professionals. Being disciplined includes knowing when to back off and *not* do something. Be consistent. Without a doubt you will miss training sessions, but if you're more consistent than not you will succeed. Green Protocol uses an incremental progression so that missing a session or two won't throw you off track or force you to repeat workouts. The less experienced you are the more consistent you should be. Consistency is probably the single most important factor for success. Turn your training into a habit like brushing your teeth.

Stay true to the goal of each session. If you're doing LSS, don't worry about speed or pace. If you're strength training don't be a hero and do a thousand burpees in between sets. Be cold, calculating, and methodical. If you're doing work capacity, strength-endurance training, or benchmark testing, be a hero. Do a thousand extra burpees, do more, push yourself. See if you can push out and hit that ultramarathon distance. Harness your inner Goggins. Point is there's a time and place for everything, don't sabotage your progress by doing the wrong thing at the wrong time.

Avoid overanalyzing and dissecting single sessions. It's a waste of time. You'll have good and bad workouts for the rest of your life for hundreds of different reasons. It doesn't matter. Gauge your success over the long term. Check in with yourself after a few months, not at the end of each session. Go to the gym or hit the trails, then forget about it. Go about the rest of your day. Tactical fitness is like the stock market. Some days you're up, some days you're down, but as long as you're rising over the long term, you're good to go.

When you get your dream job or pass that lifechanging selection, come back and share the wealth. Don't forget us. Visit the Tactical Barbell forum or subreddit and provide others on the path with insight.

KB

FAQs

What do I do if I miss a session or two?

Skip it and move on to the next workout. This program is grounded in the real world. It's specifically designed to accommodate missed sessions by using a more gradual progression spread over three week blocks. The three week block gives it a built-in redundancy. The progression is slow enough that moving on to the next workout doesn't require a great leap in ability and will give you a reset. You could probably miss one or two sessions every single week and still gain 80-90% of the benefits of this program, not that I recommend it.

What if I can't finish the weekly long run, back to backs, or long rucks?

This ties into the first question. Unlikely, but if you do it's probably because you missed a few too many sessions and got ahead of your abilities or pushed too hard when you should've been conservative. Regardless of the reason, go back to the beginning of the three week block you're on and repeat from there. For example, if you're unable to complete the back-to-back rucks during week 7 of Outcome, take your deload week, then go back and start at week 5/day 1. Similarly, if you were unable to finish the 8 mile long ruck during week 5, you'd go back to week 1/day 1. Keep repeating that 3-week chunk until you get past your problem session.

What if I don't have a hill for the hill sessions?

Try to find stairs (stadiums, apartment buildings). Continuous Hill Runs, Vertical Tempo Runs, and 2/1 Hills can all be done on the treadmill (see Session Guide). As a last resort, speedwork (Tempo Runs, Mile Repeats, Fartlek etc.) can replace Hill sessions.

I don't think I'll be able to hit next week's SE reps – should I change my baseline maximums?

No. That's the entire point of SE. Fail, get tired, and work through it. One rep at a time if you have to. SE isn't maximal-strength training. Adaptation is triggered by abbreviated rest and failure. You'll also be stronger and more adapted than you think when the next session rolls around. The only time I suggest resetting your maximums is if you're using external weight (barbells, dumbbells, weight vest) and you clearly bit off more than you can chew. In that case lower the weight as much as you like.

The weights feel too heavy during my Operator, Fighter, Zulu sessions etc.

Drop your 1RM for the unmanageable exercise by 10-15%. Or use a training max throughout for all exercises. A training max is 90% of your 1RM used as your 1RM.

I finished a block of Op, Fighter, Zulu, etc. but the weight still feels heavy on a particular exercise. Adding weight to my 1RM for the next block will make it too much for me too handle. What do I do?

Sometimes the best progression is no progression. Use the same maximum until you own it and you're ready for more. It might even take more than a block or two. Often, we expect the body to improve much more quickly than it actually does. It takes time for adaptation to occur, more or less time depending on nutrition, genetics, and recovery management.

How come there isn't more two-a-day training?

Two-a-days are great, a force multiplier. I am a strong believer in them. But again, this program is grounded in the real world. There are always exceptions, but in my experience most people can't or won't sustain consistent two-a-day training for very long. They get excited because it's something new, do it for a while, eventually stop, and their entire plan gets disrupted and thrown off. Those that can usually have a schedule or lifestyle that makes it easy – like soldiers in garrison. They're forced to PT in the mornings, and in the evenings they're eager to hit the weights on their own time. Or the ERT member that gets to PT on shift while on company time. I also believe one quality session a day is more than enough for most goals. Be consistent with less, instead of all over the place with more. That said, if you get the opportunity to add a second session, go for it.

I am one of the exceptions, I'm in a position to do two-a-days. What kind of training should I add?

LSS, LSS, LSS. 30-60 minutes or more. One of the easiest and most efficient ways to build overall work capacity and endurance. Even if you end up doing LSS twice in one day, that's a good day. Also, it's tougher to burn yourself out doing LSS if you're doing it correctly. Another option is to work on a personal weak link, like speedwork, water confidence, or a particular exercise like pull-ups etc.

Isn't weight vest running bad for you?

You'll find people in the community for and against. Consider that how you do it might matter. If you weigh yourself down like a mule with 50lbs and go for a two hour flat run on pavement, you're doing it wrong. On the other hand, if you start with a conservative 5-10lbs, jog on a trail, and break it up with some uphill hiking… You have to decide for yourself. Don't do anything you don't feel comfortable doing. Don't do anything that contradicts what your doctor tells you.

During LSS, my heartrate rockets up to 170 or higher even when I'm just walking up a hill. Should I stick to flat roads/trails?

No. Hike to the top, take a minute or two and enjoy the view. Let your heartrate settle, then continue. Your heartrate will occasionally spike on trail runs because of the terrain. You'll get fitter and fitter over time. As you do, your heartrate will sort itself out. Eventually you'll get to a point where you'll be able to jog some of those hills while staying at that low effort zone 2ish pace. The only time I recommend flat roads (and a bit of OCD when it comes to heartrate) is during Capacity.

During LSS, my heartrate goes above 150 even when I'm jogging slowly. Should I walk?

No. In this case stop using your monitor as a point of reference and use the talk-test or nasal breathing instead. Jog at a pace that allows you to speak in paragraphs, or breathe through your nose to control your pace. When you get fitter go back to using your monitor.

Will using this program guarantee I pass selection/school/etc?

No. No program can. Physical fitness is just the price of entry. Being strong is not the same as being tough. What happens between your ears will determine how far you go. Consider that collegiate athletes freqently fail selection. Consider that 4ft9, 97lb Richard Flaherty (aka the 'Giant Killer') passed the Special Forces Q course and eventually became an SFOD commander. If you want it badly enough, you'll find a way to make it happen. Physical fitness adds to being a great operator, it doesn't equate to being a great operator.

ABOUT THE AUTHOR

KB is the pseudonym for a 25 year military and federal law enforcement member. The author has served on a variety of units; as an infantryman, paratrooper, and operator on a federal hostage rescue team.

Printed in Great Britain
by Amazon